£16 00

STANDARD LOAN

UNLESS RECALLED BY ANOTHER READER
THIS ITEM MAY BE BORROWED FOR

FOUR WEEKS

To renew, online at: http://prism.talis.com/chi-ac/
or by telephone: 01243 816089 (Bishop Otter)
01243 812099 (Bognor Regis)

- 1 NOV 2011

1 2 DEC 2011

D1334104

UNIVERSITY OF CHICHESTER
LIBRARY

WS 2245241 9

510
7
TUR

Related titles of interest

Literacy through Creativity
Prue Goodwin
(1-84312-087-9)

Creativity in the Primary Curriculum
Russell Jones and Dominic Wyse
(1-84312-871-1)

Understanding Primary Mathematics
Christine Hopkins, Sue Hope and Sandy Pepperall
(1-84312-012-7)

Mathematical Knowledge for Primary Teachers
Jennifer Suggate, Andrew Davis and Maria Goulding
(1-84312-750-2)

MAKING CONNECTIONS IN PRIMARY MATHEMATICS

A Practical Guide

SYLVIA TURNER

JUDITH McCULLOUCH

 David Fulton Publishers

David Fulton Publishers Ltd
The Chiswick Centre, 414 Chiswick High Road, London W4 5TF

www.fultonpublishers.co.uk

First published in Great Britain in 2004 by David Fulton Publishers

10 9 8 7 6 5 4 3 2 1

Note: The rights of Sylvia Turner and Judith McCullouch to be identified as the authors of this work have been asserted by them in accordance with the Copyright, Designs and Patents Act 1988.

David Fulton Publishers is a division of Granada Learning Limited, part of ITV plc.

Copyright © Sylvia Turner and Judith McCullouch 2004

British Library Cataloguing in Publication Data
A catalogue record for this book is available from the British Library.

ISBN 1-84312-088-7

All rights reserved. No part of this publication may be reproduced, stored in a retrieval system or transmitted, in any form or by any means, electronic, mechanical, photocopying, or otherwise, without the prior permission of the publishers.

25   05

CRAWLEY COLLEGE OF
TECHNOLOGY
LIBRARY

Acc. No.	Class	
387272	372.7	TUR

Typeset by RefineCatch Ltd, Bungay, Suffolk
Printed and bound in Great Britain

Contents

Acknowledgements

The idea for this book arose out of many conversations with colleagues, both teachers and lecturers, about the nature of mathematics and its teaching in primary schools.

We would like to thank:

- those who acted as sounding boards for our thoughts and ideas;
- those who read and commented on the text;
- the many children who made a contribution, especially those whose work is included.

Introduction

This book is intended to support teaching students, teachers and school managers develop their knowledge of the many connections that exist in primary mathematics and apply this to their practice. We consider, for example, connections within specific mathematical topics, connections across different themes in mathematics, connections found in written and spoken language and also connections that occur throughout the primary curriculum. We envisage that this book will be used for a resource as part of the process of planning and preparing for lessons that will extend and broaden children's understanding, knowledge and use of mathematics.

Research conducted on behalf of the Teacher Training Agency to identify effective teachers of mathematics (Askew *et al.* 1997) recognised that such teachers 'connected different areas of mathematics and different ideas in the same area of mathematics using a variety of words, symbols and diagrams'. In parallel with connections is the issue of misconceptions. This has been highlighted in recent research (Gatsby Technical Education Project 1997; NNS 2002). Some of these misconceptions involve children making false connections between varying aspects of mathematics. Knowledge of common misconceptions and awareness of how misconceptions can arise also enable the teacher to be more effective.

Connections can be made across a range of mathematical topics if themes such as equivalence are considered as the linking threads. Equivalence is referred to often in this book as it is an overarching theme to many ideas in mathematics: matching, conservation, balance, symmetry, congruence, pattern and equality. A frequently occurring issue in teaching is that of effective questioning. Questions in mathematics are of great value in helping children make connections and some useful illustrations of effective questions are provided in the National Numeracy Strategy supplementary materials of 2001 (DfES 2001). The role of questioning in teaching and learning is considered further only in Chapter 3 (to avoid repetition), but it should be remembered that it is of relevance in the teaching of all aspects of mathematics. The use of ICT, both as a tool for the teacher and as a teaching and learning resource, is discussed throughout the book, explicitly or implicitly, as an integral part of teaching.

The separate attainment targets of the National Curriculum (DfEE/QCA 1999), which determine the content of primary school mathematics, form the structure of the chapters. However, this approach can work against the connections that are being identified. The diagram (on p. ix) identifies the main content of the National Curriculum to enable you to gain an overview of the possible connections throughout the book.

The first chapter considers language. Language is the main means by which mathematics is learned and therefore by which it is taught. Skemp (1991) believes that in the early years the connection between thoughts and the spoken word are initially stronger than those between thoughts and written words or thoughts and mathematical symbols. Liebeck (1990) sees the sequence of abstraction as children having experience, using language to describe it, pictures to represent it and then symbols to make generalisations. The role of language in developing mathematical understanding is fundamental to the way ideas and concepts are explained and assimilated. It is important that teachers identify words that are ambiguous in their meaning, particularly those that are used in everyday speech and mathematics. Use of such language needs to be refined to be used accurately and this comes from having an understanding of context and purpose.

Chapters 2, 3 and 4 include using and applying mathematics as covered in the National Curriculum (DfEE/QCA 1999). Each section gives information to support understanding of mathematics followed by strategies to enhance teaching and children's learning. Although handling data is part of Ma 2 Number at Key Stage 1, it is also included in Chapter 4 with Key Stage 2.

Secure subject knowledge is essential if teachers are to make connections for children. Research suggests that many primary teachers feel insecure about mathematics and unsure about many basic mathematical concepts (Haylock and Cockburn 2003). Skemp states that concept formation is something that has to happen in the learner's mind and that concepts 'are mental models . . . that must represent common properties of past experiences which we are able to recognise on future occasions' (1991: 52). This book provides opportunities for improving personal mathematics knowledge through better understanding. This should lead to improved confidence, enabling more effective teaching.

Emphasis has been given to teaching strategies that consider the relationship between language with notation and representation. Resources are discussed that aid understanding and allow teachers to help children develop accurate mental images. The importance of relating mathematics to the real world is emphasised and relevant contexts to children are identified and explored.

We consider how children learn although we do not engage with the theories underlying the different learning styles (other sources on this subject are available). We do, however, discuss how learning can be assessed in the final part of each

Finding Connections

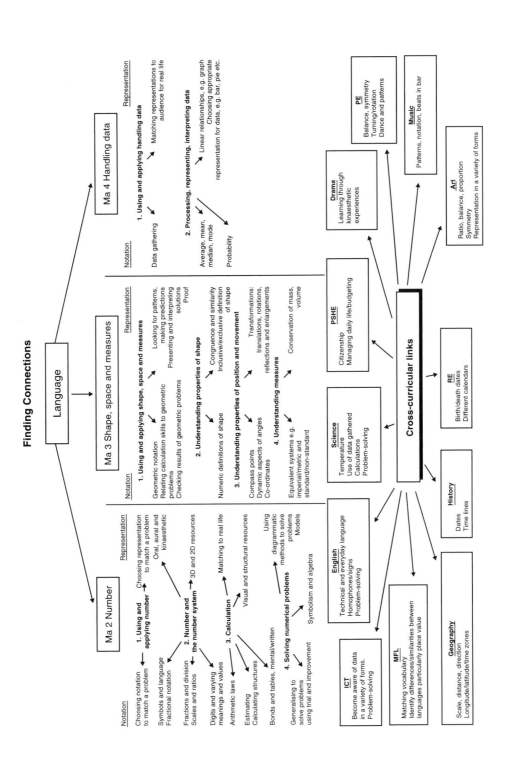

Language

Ma 2 Number

Notation — Representation

1. Using and applying number

Choosing notation to match a problem → Choosing representation to match a problem
Oral, aural and kinaesthetic

Symbols and language
Fractional notation

2. Number and the number system → 3D and 2D resources

Fractions and division
Scales and ratios → Matching to real life

Digits and varying meanings and values

Arithmetic laws

3. Calculation → Visual and structural resources

Estimating
Calculating structures

Bonds and tables, mental/written → Using diagrammatic methods to solve problems

4. Solving numerical problems → Models

Generalising to solve problems using trial and improvement → Symbolism and algebra

Ma 3 Shape, space and measures

Notation — Representation

1. Using and applying shape, space and measures

Geometric notation
Relating calculation skills to geometric problems → Looking for patterns, making predictions

Checking results of geometric problems → Presenting and interpreting solutions
Proof

2. Understanding properties of shape

Numeric definitions of shape → Congruence and similarity
Inclusive/exclusive definition of shape

3. Understanding properties of position and movement

Compass points
Dynamic aspects of angles
Co-ordinates → Transformations: translations, rotations, reflections and enlargements

4. Understanding measures

Equivalent systems e.g. imperial/metric and standard/non-standard → Conservation of mass, volume

Ma 4 Handling data

Notation — Representation

1. Using and applying handling data

Data gathering → Matching representations to audience for real life

2. Processing, representing, interpreting data

Average, mean, median, mode → Linear relationships, e.g. graph
Choosing appropriate representation for data, e.g. bar, pie etc.

Probability

Cross-curricular links

Drama
Learning through kinaesthetic experiences

PE
Balance, symmetry
Turning/rotation
Dance and patterns

Music
Patterns, notation, beats in bar

Art
Ratio, balance, proportion
Symmetry
Representation in a variety of forms

PSHE
Citizenship
Managing daily life/budgeting

RE
Birth/death dates
Different calendars

Science
Temperature
Use of data gathered
Calculations
Problem-solving

History
Dates
Time lines

English
Technical and everyday language
Homophones/signs
Problem-solving

ICT
Become aware of data in a variety of forms.
Problem-solving

MFL
Matching vocabulary
Identify differences/similarities between languages particularly place value

Geography
Scale, distance, direction
Longitude/latitude/time zones

section. Assessment can be broadly divided into two strands: assessment *for* learning and assessment *of* learning. The former is an integral part of teaching and learning which is therefore present, to varying degrees, in all lessons. It enables teachers to plan the next steps for the individual, class or group. Assessment *of* learning is a means of making summary judgements of *attainment,* which can be used to plan teaching in the long term but is particularly related to making judgements about a year group of children or a school. It should be remembered that ability and attainment are not one and the same.

We look at individual learning as advocated in the strategy for primary schools, *Excellence and Enjoyment* (DfES 2003), through consideration of a range of learning styles and modes to make learning more effective. Reference is made to assessment of children's learning from results of national testing and to an approach to addressing errors and misconceptions. We emphasise the importance of allowing children opportunities to show their understanding of mathematics as well as being involved in the assessment process themselves. The final chapter makes connections between mathematics and other curriculum subjects, again in line with *Excellence and Enjoyment.*

We hope this book will be helpful to all readers reconsidering their approach to mathematics as part of professional development.

Language

Language and semantics

Introduction

The English language is said to be a 'rich' language in that it has an extensive vocabulary derived from a wide range of influences on its development. This 'richness' means that thoughts and ideas can be expressed with clarity and subtlety, showing nuances of meaning. Take for example the word 'mean'. The idea of mean when used as an adjective can be expressed by the synonyms *selfish, nasty* or *unpleasant*. We can express unpleasantness by saying that a person is mean but not that a smell is mean. Each of these words, however, has a slightly different connotation depending on the context and interpretation. Furthermore, the word 'mean' used as a verb can show intention, e.g. *I mean to go home early today*, or the interpretation of a word, e.g. *What does 'mean' mean?* 'Mean' used as a noun in a mathematical context as a technical term has yet another quite distinct definition: the arithmetic mean is a particular type of average used in statistics.

Mathematical language includes many examples of synonyms that children must be able to understand. In everyday language, they will need to develop an understanding of the subtlety in the difference in meaning depending on context and interpretation. In mathematics, children also need to develop an understanding of the differences between mathematical synonyms. The terms *subtract, minus, take away, decrease by, the difference between* and *less than* identify the operation of subtraction but do not all refer to the same subtraction structure. Children need to be aware of these structures in order to make sense of the words used to describe them. Such synonyms and phrases related to the operation of subtraction are discussed in detail in the next chapter ('Calculation', p. 36).

Issues of understanding related to language are identified particularly with respect to children for whom English is an additional language (EAL) but these issues can relate to all children to some degree. 'Richness' of language can lead to confusion in the initial stages when children are acquiring language and developing mathematical concepts. Two other factors compound further the problem of understanding the language of mathematics. The first is the infrequent use of many mathematical terms even within the subject itself (e.g. *congruent*) which results in a lack of regular reinforcement of understanding. Secondly, mathematical terminology is often used inaccurately, e.g. *the bigger half.*

Your mathematics

First, it is useful to consider just the words or phrases with equivalent meanings and when they are introduced to children. Taking vocabulary from the National Numeracy Strategy (NNS) (DfEE 1999), it can be seen in Figure 1.1 that much of the language related to equivalence is introduced in the reception class. Skemp (1991) identifies this as an early stage in children's development of language when connections between thoughts and the spoken word are stronger than between thoughts and the written or symbolic representation.

R	1	2	3	4	5	6
make	equal to	stands for	equation	inverse	equivalent	equally
total	equals	represents		translation	reduced to	likely
sum		exact/ly			cancel	equal
altogether		round			fair	chance
is the same as		reflection			congruent	fifty-fifty
match					convert	
symmetrical						

Figure 1.1

Language is the means by which we describe our mathematical experiences. It involves the use of *both* mathematical terminology and terminology that is associated with explanation and instruction. A teacher therefore needs to ensure that the language used has a shared meaning – without shared meaning children are likely to develop misconceptions by making *false* connections or not being able to access explanations. This means being aware of language that is ambiguous. Such ambiguity can be identified in the following ways:

- Meaning that differs according to whether the word is used as a noun or a verb. For example: the word *note* can mean an instruction [verb], a form of currency [noun] *and* a musical symbol [noun].

- Words that are derived from the same root but that have a different meaning in an everyday context, e.g. the *net* of a shape and a fishing *net*. Some words in this category have two or more mathematical meanings that are used in a mathematical context (e.g. *left* denotes direction and also identifies a numerical remainder).

- Homophones and homonyms, e.g. one/won; count/Count *Ferdinand*.

Think of some words that you use commonly when teaching mathematics and consider the alternative meanings that children could derive from them. It may be helpful to look at some planning material you have used.

The way in which words are contextualised gives meaning and understanding to the complex nature of the English language but this comes with experience and use of language. Again the majority of such words are introduced early in Key Stage 1 (see Fig. 1.3). Children with EAL will have even less experience to help them to discriminate between varying uses of words than those whose first language is English.

Your teaching

Children who are not hearing-impaired experience language initially by the spoken word. When language is used as the medium to instruct or explain and label mathematical concepts, rather than for acquisition, effective teaching will depend on variables such as children's preferred learning styles. In order to meet the needs of the majority of children in a class, they need to be offered a variety of ways to learn language.

Ambiguities

The following strategies aim to support the understanding of mathematical language to accommodate different learning styles and modes as well as to support children with EAL and those with a hearing impairment. Teaching needs to take into consideration misconceptions associated with language. Planning should include identification of possible ambiguity in the language that is to be used and teaching strategies should be devised that take such language into account. The topic of fractions can be used to illustrate strategies to deal with possible ambiguity:

- Avoid using an ambiguous word when **introducing** a concept, e.g. *whole/hole*. It is not helpful to completely avoid ambiguous terminology – children need to be aware of words that can have different meanings as this knowledge will eventually enable them to consider carefully a range of meanings and apply them appropriately:

  *I have a **whole** pizza* [use of real or replica pizza for visual understanding]
  How much pizza do I have?
  What is another way of saying I have a whole pizza? [all of it; complete pizza etc.]

● Make explicit the false connection and invent rhymes to help children to be aware and remember the difference in meaning:

A whole egg doesn't have any holes.

> Make up rhymes using homophones that can be associated with mathematics (see Fig. 1.3). It is useful to illustrate the rhymes.

● Model the use of language and reinforce with a range of teaching strategies including 'real-life' examples:

Two halves make one whole.

Demonstrate cutting of shapes into two equal parts and putting back together again (Fig. 1.2) – ensure that the shapes are not all circular or hole-like!

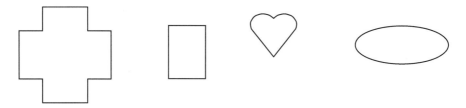

Figure 1.2

● Present children with experiences or questions that may expose language misconceptions which can lead to discussion, thereby making them receptive to challenging their own misconceptions:

Draw me a whole pizza.
Do pizzas have to be round? [point to the pictures that show whole shapes]
Use a variety of prototypes or examples of equivalent but different visual images to represent the word 'whole'.

● Make a list of pre-prepared key words and words that you have previously identified at the planning stage as having potential for misunderstanding. Simultaneously, use structural and visual resources to demonstrate both the language of instruction and mathematics.

● Give children opportunities to repeat new words you have introduced and to articulate in their own words explanations that have been given.

● Make available written instructions or picture clues so that children can refer to them if they are unable to remember spoken instructions.

● Develop an interactive approach to teaching that encourages children to actively participate through a range of techniques – giving explanations, writing responses or manipulating resources.

- Allow for a variety of responses in mathematical activities – written recording, verbal explanation, written explanation and demonstration.

- Allow children opportunities to work in pairs, in small groups or as a class so that they can listen and use spoken language to develop mathematical understanding.

- Label mathematical resources so that children become familiar with the written word.

- Allow opportunities for non-directed or discovery activities that encourage children to use either written or spoken language to offer descriptions and explanations.

- Encourage children to create personal mathematics dictionaries of definitions as they begin to understand words and see them being used in different ways.

By identifying language that can cause confusion at the planning stage many misconceptions can be avoided – the children will not have to 'unlearn' false connections later. If children have already developed such misconceptions then remedial action will be needed. You will need to use the children's recorded work and question the children – they will not necessarily be aware themselves of what aspect of language they misunderstand and misconceptions may not manifest themselves immediately. Take, for example, the language of multiplication. By Year 2, children will be introduced to a range of equivalent terms for this operation: *lots of, groups of, times, multiply* as well as the relationship to *repeated addition*. This means that they will need to know the different terminology for the same operation and the structures they represent *and* have an awareness of the equivalence between calculating by multiplying and by adding. They will also require a clear understanding of the individual words, e.g. they should not confuse the word 'times' with 'time' in its sense of measurement.

Figure 1.3 should help in this process of both trying to avoid misconceptions and remedying them. The list is by no means complete, but it does provide an indication of the language that can be introduced in the primary school and the possible meanings that children could derive from the words. It is also worth considering the effect of pronunciation and current semantic changes in the meaning of words, e.g. side/size and net/Inter*net*.

The children's learning

Most assessment of children's language related to mathematics will be made from their responses to mathematical activity. It is important that children have the opportunities to use mathematical vocabulary themselves. Allowing time for discussion in small groups and encouraging children to use correct terminology when giving explanations fosters understanding of language. Some aspects of understanding can be assessed more explicitly in the Foundation Stage and Key Stage 1 by drawing and role-play. Children can demonstrate their understanding of words as in the following sentence: 'I ate eight apples when I went to a party.'

I ate eight apples

By Bethan   Age 5

Summary

- The 'richness' of the English language means that many words used in the teaching of mathematics have a different everyday and mathematical meaning.

- Teachers need to ensure that the language they employ has a shared meaning by using teaching strategies that take account of the differing meanings of words and of the context in which mathematics is presented.

- Teachers can avoid children developing misconceptions associated with language if potentially confusing language is identified at the planning stage.

Vocabulary	Homophone	Homonym	Everyday/ mathematical
acute	a[cute]		
and			= add **conjunction**
bottom			lowest part **body part**
count		**Count [of Monte Cristo]**	
cross			identifying movement or identifying particular attribute **angry** **letter – X**
degree			measurement of angle measurement of temperature **academic qualification**
difference			attribute **[including everyday use]** subtract
draw	drawer		
eight	ate		
even			**level** **Even when he . . .**
face			surface of shape **present/turn to** **front of head**
fair [impartial]	fare	fair [fairground] fair – pale	
feet/foot			imperial measurement **body part**
figures			numbers shape/form
flat			2D **even** **place to live**
hour	our		
key	quay		
left			direction – it is on the left **[including everyday use]** remainder – what is left **verb – she left today**
make/s	'		equal **make a cake**

Vocabulary	Homophone	Homonym	Everyday/ mathematical
match			join **game [football]** **match [that you strike]**
mean			average **poor** **unpleasant**
metre	meter [gas]		
minus			4 minus 1 If the temperature is minus 4 it is very cold.
minute		minute [tiny]	
net			of shape **for fishing**
note			to write down currency
odd			**strange**
one	won		
operation			of arithmetic **medical**
pair	pear		
[per] cent	scent		of a hundred but relates to fractional quantity and currency
plane	plain		**abbreviation for aeroplane**
positive			not negative **[also of electricity]** **definite**
pound			currency **hit**
present [show]		present – gift	
prime			number **perfection**
product			quantity derived from multiplying quantities together **result of process of manufacture**
proper/ improper			**correct/incorrect**
property			attribute **building**
record		record [vinyl disc]	write down **tape [verb]** **facts known**

Vocabulary	Homophone	Homonym	Everyday/ mathematical
relationship			connection of attributes **connections between people**
right	write wright rite		direction – it is on the right **[including everyday use]** **= correct** **= just**
roll			throw [as with die] **move round** **shape of bread**
rough[ly] = estimation		rough = not smooth	
route	root		
row		row [argument]	
rule			as with ruler **school rules**
ruler		ruler [person in charge]	
scales			use in measuring **part of fish**
second			ordinal number unit for measuring time
set			group **tennis score** **set [as in jelly]**
slide **in**			move [as in transforming shapes] **and** **everyday use** **slide in hair** **slide in play park**
spring		spring [season]	**upward movement**
symbol	cymbal		
table			tabular form **piece of furniture**
take away			subtraction calculation **convenience meal [as in Chinese takeaway]**
time/s			3 times 4 Tell me the time.

Vocabulary	Homophone	Homonym	Everyday/ mathematical
volume			capacity of a 3D shape based upon its dimensions denotes quantity but often associated with degree of sound **one in a series of books**
weight	wait		
whole	hole		
yard			imperial measurement **plot [builder's or garden]**

Figure 1.3 Mathematics vocabulary list. *Note:* this list has been selected from the vocabulary identified by the National Numeracy Strategy (DfEE 1999). Often the origin of the word is the same but its current use has been modified, e.g. *match* – to join, put against. (**Bold** type indicates everyday use.)

The language of near equivalence

Introduction

Just as children need to develop an understanding of the subtlety in the difference in meaning of synonyms – as well as an awareness of the range of homophones and homonyms used when mathematics is taught – they also need to develop an understanding of the language of near equivalence as it relates to context and interpretation.

Appreciation of context is fundamental to an understanding of near equivalence in language. In the reception year, children are introduced to the words *nearly, close to* and *about the same* when counting, estimating and comparing both contexts of number and measurement. Progression in correct use of the language of near equivalence comes from awareness that in measurement there must be a level of accuracy in a concept that intrinsically is not accurate, and in number an understanding that an emotional response is related to numerical response when calculating near equivalence:

It's nearly time to go home.
I'm nearly a metre tall.
I've written about the same as Jack.

Your mathematics

It can be seen from Figure 1.4 that much of this language is introduced in reception classes when children are still at the early stages of language development.

R	1	2	3	4	5	6
nearly close to about the same as just over just under	roughly	approximate/ly		greater than or equal to less than or equal to is approximately equal to	likely certain probable chance	

Figure 1.4

A child may say he is nearly five years old because he interprets that, from his experience, it is a positive thing to reach this great age. So saying 'I'm nearly five' would be an expected response. Similarly, taking a different, if related, context of number such as counting, a child who is making a set of objects, e.g. sand pies in a tray of sand, may say he has nearly five pies if that is his given target number:

Jack, I want you to make me five sand pies this morning [Jack sets about the task quickly, wanting to please].
I've nearly made five [still making third sand pie].

Although it will again be viewed as something positive to attain, it does not necessarily relate to accuracy in numeracy but more an emotional response for a desired goal.

Your teaching

Initially children in the reception year and Key Stage 1 need to become more objective in using the language of near equivalence. Contexts that are not directly related to the children themselves will encourage such objectivity (Fig. 1.5).

Personal contexts	Impersonal contexts
Sand pies etc. made by child	Objects arranged in sets for comparison
Items personally brought to school by child	Cards with symbols, e.g. dots
Measures related to child e.g. height	Measures of objects in the classroom
Comparison of child's objects/cards with another child e.g. Has Jack got more than you?	Use of equipment, e.g. 2 pan balance

Figure 1.5

An increased ability to make sensible estimations is needed for children to be able to develop the concept of rounding. Children will start to use the concept of rounding to multiples of 10 in a range of contexts, e.g.:

- The mental mathematics strategy of adjusting by 1 when adding or subtracting 9 or 11 which, in Key Stage 2, leads into compensating by adding too much or subtracting a quantity to aid calculation such as in the following example:

727 + 97 = 727 + 100 – 3 = 824

- The concept of rounding to check calculations:

74 + 37 can be rounded to the nearest ten 70 + 40 which equals 110 so the answer should be about 110.

- The idea of rounding in problem-solving contexts, particularly when dealing with remainders:

> The school has planned a trip to the zoo. There are 220 children in the school and coaches hold 60 children. How many coaches will be needed?

Contexts for such numerical problems are extended into the sphere of measurement when children start to use measuring equipment with scales to measure length, mass, capacity and temperature and interpret the results.

> Identify an age range and consider contexts in which children can be introduced to appropriate measures of near equivalence.

By the end of Key Stage 2, a developed sense of the language of near equivalence is necessary if children are to be able to understand that 1012 can be approximately 1000 in the context of winning £1012 in the lottery or estimating the cost of a holiday but not when paying a bill.

Probability is an aspect of mathematics that identifies what is or is not likely. This depends upon personal experience as well as data that can be used for calculation. Therefore an awareness of the relationship between personal responses to the language of near equivalence needs to be discussed with children. Time is also a useful topic for this purpose as many phrases are open to a range of interpretation:

I'll see you about 2 o'clock.
It's nearly 2 o'clock.

So it can be seen that an awareness of the context with which a child is presented with the language of near equivalence is important if they are not to develop misconceptions across the mathematics curriculum. Teachers need to plan appropriate contexts for children to develop this understanding so that they are able to refine their use of the language of near equivalence.

The children's learning

Below is an example of work that led from a discussion about examples of four terms denoting near equivalence – *nearly, close to, just under* and *just over*. The children were asked to consider these terms and put them in a sentence to show what they thought the words meant. Although there were just two scribes, all three children contributed to the discussion. It can be seen that the children understood the terms in both numerical and spatial contexts.

Nearly

Close to

Just over

Just under

the car I sheard
there
the cat is close to the
mouse
the house is appus
over then pillo

I am nearly 3.
I am just under 3.
I am just over five

I am close to 6.

Kaylah, Freddie and Kitty, aged 5

Summary

- The language of near equivalence is introduced at an early stage in a child's mathematical teaching.
- The context in which the language of near equivalence is used affects its meaning.
- Teachers need to plan contexts for children to develop an appropriate understanding of the language of near equivalence.

CHAPTER 2

Number

SOME KEY CONNECTIONS WITHIN AND ACROSS ATTAINMENT TARGETS

- Using and applying mathematics as an integrated teaching and learning strategy throughout all elements of the mathematics curriculum.
- Use of digits in differing contexts with consideration of meaning and value.
- Calculation structures.
- Arithmetic laws and their use in solving calculations with both whole and fractional quantities.
- Fractional forms.
- Fractional notation and probability.
- Negative numbers and temperature scales.
- Mental and written methods of calculation.
- Choice of calculation strategies dependent on the examples chosen.
- Symbols that represent instruction and value.

Using and applying number

Introduction

What do you understand is meant by 'using and applying' number? Teachers and students to whom we have spoken are often unsure about this attainment target but in many ways it is the basis of all teaching of number. Why learn to calculate in school if you cannot use or apply this knowledge to other aspects of mathematics, the curriculum and out-of-school contexts?

The problem in teaching using and applying number often relates to the terminology surrounding it. Such phrases as 'communicate in spoken, written and pictorial form' or 'understand a general statement' are not specific in terms of content. 'Understand multiplication as repeated addition' and 'find remainders after division' immediately conjure up ideas about the type of content to be taught.

When discussing using and applying mathematics with teaching students, they often ask 'Do you mean problem-solving and investigations?' almost immediately wanting something tangible to think about. However, although problem-solving and investigations are part of using and applying mathematics (and this will be discussed in detail later in this chapter), there are more fundamental concepts to be considered involving the main focus of this book – making connections. The National Curriculum explicitly identifies the making of connections at the beginning of each Key Stage: 'Teaching should ensure that appropriate connections are made between the sections on number, shape, space and measures and handling data' (DfEE/QCA 1999).

If children are genuinely to use and apply number, they need to connect much of the number work they learn in school to:

- other aspects of mathematics;
- other curriculum subjects;
- the wider world.

To do this, teachers need to know these connections and the skills necessary to acquire them before they can make them accessible to children. Mathematics cannot be seen in terms of merely content but connections can only be made explicit in terms of content. The skills children need to acquire in order to use and apply number are making connections by:

- reasoning;
- communicating;
- developing a range of strategies to find solutions.

Every mathematics lesson can involve opportunities for using and refining these skills. The first two skills involve language in part. Strategies for finding solutions require children to use language and relate it to equivalent notation and representation. How do they learn to do this?

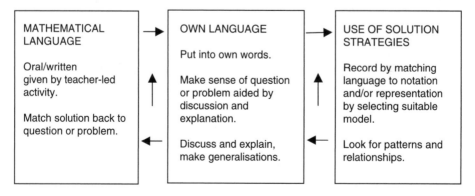

Figure 2.1

Communicating, reasoning and problem-solving result initially from the way children are taught and how they learn from these experiences.

Your mathematics

So what subject knowledge do you need to have in using and applying number so you feel secure in what you are teaching and how to teach it? Knowledge required to teach the other attainment targets has been included in the relevant sections but, as has been already stated, there is no specific body of knowledge associated with this attainment target.

Knowledge for using and applying

The knowledge comes from the skills and understanding required to make connections in number:

- understanding of progression in developing skills of communication, reasoning and problem-solving in children;
- understanding of the language associated with number;
- awareness of the resources, diagrams and models that can be used to represent number;
- awareness of how such language and representations connect to notation.

A useful starting point is to look at how you developed these skills and understanding. You may feel you are still struggling to develop them!

Consider the mathematics you use on a day-to-day basis – budgeting, checking bank statements and looking for the best value in household purchases or a holiday. How do you set about the task? Do you make rough estimates first, work alone or discuss the task with someone else? Do you draw diagrams and/or jottings or carry out standard calculations?

This may lead you on to consider how you learnt mathematics and what strategies worked for you and what did not. People learn in different ways. Some learn by doing, others by reading, following diagrams or observing and some prefer to have verbal explanations. Most people, however, learn by a combination of methods. It is this awareness that will help develop your understanding of how children learn and how your teaching can develop their understanding (mathematical reasoning is discussed in Chapter 3, 'Using and applying shape, space and measures', p. 59).

Your teaching

Language, notation and representation

Fundamental to effective learning is the need to make teaching accessible. Teachers have to use a range of strategies in order to do this, taking into account different learning styles. Just as in learning to read, children need to connect the spoken word to the concept it represents and then to the written word, so children have to connect numbers. Take, for example, just a single-digit number such as four. Children need to evoke several knowledge and understanding skills. Look at Figure 2.2 to see how the number four can be interpreted and represented.

Aural	Visual or tactile either in form of picture or object or as a mental image.	Visual symbol and/or word	Oral
'four' **** ♡♡♡♡ four or for? ⬜⬜⬜⬜		4 four	'four'

Figure 2.2

Children then have to select an appropriate aspect of the concept of a number. Does the four relate to its place, as in 'four-hundred and twenty-one', and what context does it relate to? Is it the nominal, cardinal or ordinal aspect of the number? (This is discussed further in 'Number and the number system' below.)

> Think of the images that are evoked when you hear the word *half*. It may be you see the notation $1/2$ or it may be the written word. Alternatively you may see an image of a diagram or an object such as a cake.

Frequently, children are taught through verbal interaction but have to respond by writing or using resources. If the teacher does not relate teaching to written responses or resources by modelling and demonstrating during verbal interaction then children are not necessarily going to make the connections to notation and representation.

As has been stated in Chapter 1, language is the means by which mathematical ideas are communicated. So a starting point is to look at the language used in using and applying number. Are the words or phrases you, as the teacher, used ambiguous or misleading? Children have to learn to interpret language themselves by being taught different or confusing meanings of words. Initially, however, questions and problems need to be phrased to take account of such ambiguity. Instructions and explanations need to be clear.

Take the question a teacher may ask a child: 'Give me a number bigger than 4?' First, the child has to interpret the question by making sense of it. What is required? Does the teacher literally mean 'give' or does 'give' mean 'tell/say'? What does bigger mean? Is it a spatial question or to do with numerical (cardinal) value as illustrated in Figure 2.3?

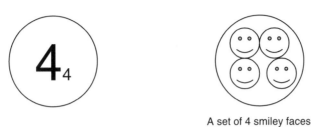

A set of 4 smiley faces

Figure 2.3

The child then has to find a solution. Sharing their answer with the person sitting next to them can help to develop the child's confidence to 'have a go'. Interaction in the form of questioning, discussing and explaining to both peers and teacher will develop the skills of reasoning and communicating. Your skill comes from asking questions that encourage children to apply knowledge they have already acquired and explain their thinking.

Consider again the question about a number bigger than 4. Some children may be able to find a solution from just spoken language by counting on from 4 – 'five, six, seven' etc. and so will have a range of solutions. Others will have to connect their sense of the question with notation and/or a representation. What is important here is the necessity for children to realise that there is equivalence between the language of number, notation and representation. Spoken 'four' may require to be matched with symbol 4. The position of 4 needs to be seen in its ordinal context, i.e. in relation to other numbers and numbers that are identified as being bigger. Children can 'see' either in the form of visual resources showing the notation or from a mental image developed through the use of visual resources as demonstrated in the number line in Figure 2.4.

1	2	3	**4**	5	6	7	8	9	10

Figure 2.4

A solution may then be found. If a child cannot relate the question to language or notation, a representation needs to be connected to the question. This representation could be two- or three-dimensional. Some number lines show both notation and icons in the form of pictures or shapes, e.g. circles or towers of bricks. 'Bigger' then has a real meaning for a child as it relates to an identifiable value as seen by the representation. Similarly, towers of bricks can be used to represent the numbers and again the value of the numbers has a visual, spatial property.

Think of a question you may ask a child relating to number. It may help to look at some past planning to give you some ideas and a context. What connections would you expect a child to make to the language involved, including false connections? Consider the range of images and resources that a child may use to find a solution and the support you could offer.

As children progress from counting, using and recognising numerals up to ten to larger numbers, patterns and number operations, so the range of opportunities to use and apply number increase. They need to be given experiences that allow them to approach problems involving number in a variety of ways and make connections across their increasing mathematical knowledge. Initially, the teacher needs to make these connections for them by such strategies as:

- Referring back to previous work: apart from verbal reminders, retaining and displaying simple planning overview grids of work each week can also reinforce this.

- Asking questions that encourage children to communicate and explain connections, e.g. *Have you seen this symbol before? Can you think of another way to record this?*

- Asking questions that encourage children to offer a range of answers and/or solutions: *What is the same/different about this set of numbers? Can you think of two/three etc. numbers that will give the answer 24 when they are multiplied together?*

In this way children are learning to use and apply number every day. Closed questions have a value but can limit the opportunities children have to extend their thinking. Teachers are sometimes reluctant to ask open questions because they are insecure in their own knowledge but this can be overcome by careful planning and preparation.

Choice of appropriate numbers is also a key factor in effective teaching.

Why is 24 a good choice of number? Can you think of any other numbers that would suit the same purpose?

This ensures that children have frequent opportunities to use and apply their knowledge and solve problems in other mathematical topics, curriculum subjects and the outside world.

Again, weekly planning overview grids that identify all curriculum subjects can help you to identify possible connections across the curriculum. Homework is an ideal opportunity to encourage children to use and apply their knowledge.

Methods of calculation

It takes time to develop understanding of the equivalence and efficiency of methods of calculation. It is, however, fundamental to using and applying mathematics. When children were taught just one method and were required to apply it regardless of the context or the numbers involved they had limited opportunity to make decisions and apply their knowledge.

> A car travels 280 kilometres in $3^{1}/_{2}$ hours. What is the average speed per hour? Compare your method of calculation with that of two or three other people. Which method was the most efficient? Would you alter your method if the numbers changed?

By Key Stage 2, children need to have been encouraged to develop a style of working that they apply instinctively: checking work, choosing resources and providing opportunities for discussion need to be considered when planning teaching. This should be done first from a practical consideration:

- Can children easily access resources?
- Are support staff aware of how children need to develop independence?

Other questions that may need to be asked involve:

- The social context, e.g. do children have the opportunity to discuss their work with peers and/or an adult?
- Emotional context, e.g. does the task motivate the child/ren and is the timetable sufficiently flexible that children pursue the task to its conclusion?
- Learning styles, modes and special educational needs (SEN) – is the required response to the task sufficiently flexible that it allows children to work and demonstrate understanding in a variety of ways?

Misconceptions

Misconceptions that can arise in using and applying mathematics usually relate to children making false generalisations. Examples relating to number include those that arise from children applying observations of concepts in one context to another. For example, multiplication with whole numbers leads to the understanding that the result is always a larger number. However, when multiplication is applied to fractional quantities the 'rule' no longer works:

multiplication makes the answer bigger (than the numbers being multiplied)

$6 \times 2 = 12$ but $6 \times 0.5 = 3$

False generalisations are formed also by choice of example:

$2^2 = 4$ so $3^2 = 6$ by doubling or 9 by squaring?

As both doubling and squaring 2 result in 4, this would be a confusing first example of index notation to use, even though the numbers are small.

Avoidance of such examples is not necessarily a means of taking children's learning forward as long as the teacher is aware of such false generalisations. Such examples may be used actively to check children's understanding and develop discussion. Fundamental to progress is finding solutions to problems, being able to communicate and to reason when confronted with knowledge that does not fit a child's current understanding. The constructivist perspective suggests that children who are offered experiences that challenge their knowledge will then adapt their ideas to incorporate this new knowledge and so further develop their understanding.

The children's learning

Children need opportunities to use and apply number every day – it cannot simply be ticked off in a box as completed. It is useful if children know that is what they are engaged in through explicit involvement with the process of inclusion of using and applying number within their mathematics lesson.

One way of doing this is to rephrase teaching objectives in 'childspeak' language. For example, 'Choose and use appropriate number operations and appropriate ways of calculating to solve problems' (NNS Teaching Programme Year 4, DfEE 1999) can be rephrased as 'I can choose the right operation when I do word problems and I can find a good way of working it out.' If we consider how we know that we have learnt something it usually fits into one of the following categories:

- you can explain to someone else;
- you can use it and be successful not once but a number of times;
- you can apply knowledge so it is automatic – you just know it.

Using the analogy of learning to drive, skills such as changing gear can become divorced from road sense. Just as there is little point being able to make a car move if other road users and traffic systems are not considered, there is little point having knowledge of calculation methods unless you can use and apply them. An issue to consider is whether children learn or you teach skills in isolation and then apply them to questions, problems and investigations or whether you present children with questions, problems and investigations and then look for solutions.

Summary

- Using and applying number can be taught discretely in the form of problem-solving and investigations but only when children have been given opportunities on a regular basis in mathematics to develop the skills needed.

- Teaching of the skills of reasoning, communicating and developing solving strategies should be part of every lesson.

- Children need to be taught to make connections between language, notation and representation by teachers modelling solution strategies.

- The experiences of number should not be isolated to number lessons but need to be drawn from school-based activity in mathematics and other subjects, as well as the wider world, so that children can connect their learning experiences and so use and apply number.

Number and the number system

Introduction

Number is a concept of quantity. Our first introduction to number comes from everyday experiences that we learn to describe. Words such as 'lots' or 'more' are used to describe toys, sweets and other familiar objects in relation to the objects we have or want in our possession. In this way, children experience numbers through their senses of sight, hearing and touch and then have to connect these with a number system that is complex. They are presented with a wide variety of notation and representation that appears equivalent but can have varying meaning depending on its relationship to place and context. Therefore knowledge and understanding of the number system is fundamental to making sense of number.

Your mathematics

We use the Hindu-Arabic number system. This evolved from the ancient Hindu system that was developed by Arab traders in the ninth and tenth centuries and spread through Europe. The strength of the system is that it has just ten symbols with the addition of two symbols to denote negative and positive worth to make all values. 0, 1, 2, 3, 4, 5, 6, 7, 8, 9, –, +. The values are made up using a complex system of altering the value of the symbol according to place – **place value**. Any one symbol can have a variety of values dependent on its place in relation to other symbols: 3, 30, 300 etc. Each place increases value by a power of 10 to the left (and inversely decreases value by a factor of 10 to the right).

This system develops beyond the counting or **natural** numbers to include negative numbers: –3, –30, –300 etc. Together, the natural numbers, negative numbers and zero are called **integers**. Fractional notation in decimal forms, e.g. 0.3, 0.03, 0.003 etc. as well as in the form $3/10$, $3/100$, $3/1000$ or $3:10$, $3:100$ $3:1000$ etc. are **rational** numbers as they are numbers that are the ratio of two integers. Another group of numbers includes those which cannot be written as the ratio of two whole numbers. These are known as **irrational** numbers. For example, there is no number that can be squared (i.e. multiplied by itself) that will give the exact answer 2, therefore $\sqrt{2}$ is an irrational number. The decimal expansion of an **irrational** number is infinite. Also, numbers can be considered as real or imaginary. Whole numbers, fractions and irrational numbers are all **real**. A **real** number is a number that can be written out as a decimal, even though it might take for ever to do so. But **imaginary** numbers cannot; something has to lie on the ordinary one-dimensional number line in order to be real. For example, we notice that −1 and other negative numbers don't have square roots. But sometimes it would be very useful if every number had a square root. So we **imagine** that there is a number, called i, which is defined by saying that when you square it you get −1.

Other terminology that you need to understand relating to number properties is listed below:

- Odd – a natural number that does not have 2 as a factor, e.g. 1, 3, 5, 7 etc.
- Even – a natural number that does have 2 as a factor, e.g. 2, 4, 6, 8 etc.
- Multiple – the result of multiplying a number by an integer 4 (4×1), 8 (4×2), 12 (4×3) etc.
- Factor – an integer that divides another integer exactly, e.g. the factors of 6 are 1, 2, 3 and 6.
- Prime – an integer that can only be divided by itself and 1, e.g. 2, 3, 5, 7, 11, etc. A prime number must have two factors therefore the number 1 is not a prime number.
- Square – a number multiplied by itself or 'squared', e.g. 4 (2×2).
- Cube – a number multiplied by itself twice, e.g. 8 ($2 \times 2 \times 2$).

> Write down some numbers – e.g. your date of birth 15.10.61. How many different number properties of these numbers can you find?

Your teaching

Connections between notation and representation need to be made explicit to children through choice of examples, resources and explanations.

| Notation | Representation |

Early number and counting: concepts and symbolism

The fundamental character of a symbol is that it stands for something else, e.g. £ represents pounds sterling. Mathematics uses many symbols that enable us to manipulate mathematical concepts. The first mathematical symbols that children probably encounter are the symbols 1, 2, 3, 4 etc. These symbols stand for the concept of the counting or natural numbers. Confusion can arise, as the symbols can look different.

If children are learning to recognise and write numbers they will initially need to have the opportunity of making their own representations of symbols with materials such as Playdoh and plasticine. They can trace the symbol in sand and on paper. They also need to have experience of the symbol from real-life examples in the environment such as door numbers, newsprint etc.

Taking four as an example, these are just some of the ways in which children will be presented with the symbol. These experiences of the symbol will come from both the wider world and school. Just as children need to understand the concept of a colour by first classifying objects regardless of the shade, so they need to begin to understand the equivalence between variations of the symbol. Children then have to learn the relationships between the symbols in order to develop understanding of mathematical concepts.

Children need practical experience matching objects to each other. They can match number names to objects in a set (Fig. 2.5).

They need opportunities to develop their understanding of conservation of number by counting objects placed near each other and then placed over a larger area (Fig. 2.6).

Figure 2.5

Figure 2.6

The ability to recite number names correctly does not necessarily imply the ability to count. The context in which a symbol is used can affect its meaning. Take the following examples.

The meaning of 4 on a bus has nothing to do with value but is merely the name of the bus. This is the nominal aspect of the symbol.

Nominal numbers as labels

Figure 2.7

The four teddies show a set of four things. This denotes the cardinal aspect of the symbol. Children have to become aware that 4 can be attributed to any set of four objects.

Figure 2.8

Each representation of the set can be connected to its cardinal value with the appropriate numeral symbol.

The number 4 when it is used for ordering as in a race (4th) shows the ordinal aspect of number.

Figure 2.9

Finding pages in a book, the date on a calendar is made easier when one knows the order of the numbers and so emphasises the ordinal aspect of number.

There is also another aspect to ordinal number. Four on a clock relates to its position in relation to other numbers, e.g. 4 comes between 3 and 5. Children need to develop an understanding of the relationship between ordinal and cardinal numbers. When they count a set of objects they are using the ordinal

Figure 2.10

aspect of number but the last number spoken gives the cardinal number for the set of objects. Using a wide range of examples from both school and the wider world can reinforce development of these three aspects of number. They will begin to grasp the ordinal aspect of the natural numbers by their relationship when they are recorded and by the order in which they are spoken and so develop the idea that a symbol to the left of another symbol or that is spoken before is less than that symbol. 1, 2, 3 – symbol to the left of 3 is 2 so 2 is less than 3.

> Consider again your date of birth. Is this nominal, cardinal or ordinal? Do different parts of the date characterise different aspects of number? If you are unsure say it out loud.

Visual resources such as number lines, 100 squares and board games also emphasise the ordinal aspect of number.

> Think of resources that can be used to develop children's understanding of the use of:
> ● nominal
> ● cardinal
> ● ordinal
> numbers:

$$1\ 2\ 3\ 4$$

4 is on the right of 3 so its value is one **more** than 3

$$4\ 3$$

3 is on the right of 4 but it is worth **less** than 4

This can cause misconceptions later when children consider the order or place of the symbols in relation to each other in the base ten place value system. Rather than the number to the left being less it increases by a factor of 10.

Counting, properties of number and sequences

Once children have learnt to count reliably they need to identify properties of numbers in order to classify them – odd, even, multiples, factors and later prime factors and square numbers. They also need to be able to double and halve numbers and recognise near doubles such as 4 and 5. It is important to realise that numbers have properties in the same way as shapes.

100 squares enable children to see patterns such as odd and even.

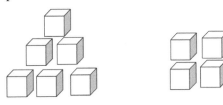

Figure 2.11

Figure 2.11 shows how manipulating cubes enables children to have a visual image of properties such as square and

27

triangle numbers. Also, this enables children to compare doubles and near doubles. Knowledge of factors and multiples can be further consolidated when working with fractions.

Place of symbol

Place value
As children develop their understanding of the cardinal aspect of number the place of the number becomes increasingly significant. As stated above, our number system is based on a complex but concise system of symbols to give all values.

Number lines including decimals, number squares – by using 100 squares children can investigate patterns, looking at where digits change value according to place. Use of electronic sources of number squares is very helpful to get children to highlight patterns, fill in missing values and make their own 100 squares.

Use of the symbols more than > and less than < and their relationship to the equals sign helps children consider place value and aids in ordering numbers. It is also a good way of introducing the concept of transitivity. This may seem obvious but it is particularly relevant to multiples and factors.

if $a < b$ and $b < c$ then $a < c$

or

if $6 < 8$ and $8 < 10$ then $6 < 10$

or

if 2 is a factor of 6 and 6 is a factor of 36 then 2 is a factor of 36. Figure 2.12 shows one way of determining factors.

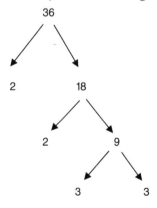

Figure 2.12

Diagrammatic methods to find factors such as factor 'trees' help children record their work systematically. Alternatively, children can work with rods such as 'colour factor'® or 'Cuisenaire'®.

Children need experience with a range of 100 squares such as 1–100, 0–99, 100–1, 99–0 in order to develop their understanding of the number system.

The role of zero as a place holder is essential to an understanding of place value. It is the purpose of the zero to make clear the position of the other digits.

In recent years there has been a move away from just representing numbers using structural apparatus such as unifix, multilink and Dienes apparatus. The rationale behind this was that children learnt to manipulate the pieces without transferring their understanding to the number system (NNS 1999).

However, some children make sense of number when they physically manipulate apparatus. Transference to the number system can be made if an equivalent form of notation is available in the form of place value digit cards. For example, a child may represent 23 using base 10 apparatus for 2 tens and 3 ones. Equivalent notation cards for 20 and 3 could then be found and overlaid so the child has a notational representation 23.

Figure 2.13 shows how the place value of the number 23 can be represented.

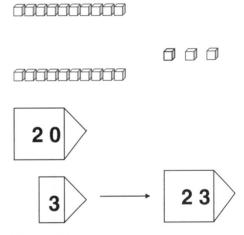

Figure 2.13

Exchange games can be played by throwing a die and building up a cumulative score, the first person to reach the target number being the winner. For example in three successive throws a child may throw a 3, a 6 and a 5. After the first two throws the total will be 9, therefore still below 10 and requiring only one column. However, after the third throw, the total will be 14, which the child can represent, in a variety of ways, as 1 ten and 4 ones. Initially, children may just use apparatus but as their understanding develops cards alone can be used.

Structural apparatus can also be placed on an overhead projector so a child can see a two-dimensional image from three-dimensional apparatus so developing their sense of an equivalent visual image. This can be further enhanced if number lines of the same dimensions are used.

Fractions

Children are first introduced to fractional quantities using the notation of common fractions such as $\frac{1}{2}$ and $\frac{1}{4}$ in Key Stage 1.

Such fractions are introduced in practical contexts using objects and diagrams. Confusion may arise if children are not able to relate the idea of a fraction beyond the representations offered to them.

Look at the diagram below and work out how many ways that you could shade it to represent one half. Think of other shapes that could be used other than squares, circles and rectangles that can be similarly shaded.

The value of 'half of' (or any fractional quantity) can only be determined when the value of the whole is known.

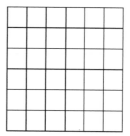

Figure 2.14

The relationship between whole numbers and fractions is made clearer by considering the ordinal aspect of fractions.

Such representations make the connection between number and shape.

Activities that emphasise fractional representations of sets of objects as well as whole objects develop understanding of fractional quantities.

Fraction notation can cause confusion for children as both parts of the fraction – the denominator and the numerator – have differing determinants for their value, e.g. $3/4$ – 3 denotes the number of parts and so involves the cardinal aspect of number and 4 denotes the type of part and could be seen as the nominal aspect of the number – the name of the fraction.

> How would you explain the different use of numbers to represent equivalent fractions such as $1/4$ and 0.25? Ensure your explanation includes reference to parts of a whole.

The relationship of the operation of division to fractional notation can also cause uncertainty when children develop the misconception that fractions relate to quantities less than 1. Again, if they are taught that a fraction is part of a quantity this is less likely to arise.

Confusion can also arise when children are introduced to the range of fractional numbers and the equivalence within and between them. Consider the following equivalent fractions $1/4$, $2/8$, $4/16$ – all equivalent but as the numbers increase the value does not. This is at odds with the experience children have when learning about and manipulating the natural numbers in the Foundation Stage and Key Stage 1.

Number lines exemplify this well and also help children relate mixed numbers to fractions.

Structural apparatus in the form of fraction walls has been traditionally used to show children the relationship between equivalent fractions. However these only work for 'families' of fractions $1/2$, $2/4$, $4/8$ and $1/3$, $2/6$, $3/9$ etc. A similar but more dynamic representation would be for children to cut overlays of paper. The top sheet would be one whole. Other sheets could be cut in strips and labelled to represent $1/2$, $2/4$, $4/8$, $1/3$, $2/6$, $3/9$ and so on. Children could not only look for equivalence between 'families' of fractions but compare fractions between 'families' and investigate how they could find out more about the relationship between, for example, a third and a half, making connections to their knowledge of factors, various visual representations of fractions and problem-solving skills.

> Think of the sets of objects that children regularly encounter that can be used to represent fractional quantities, e.g. food.

Work with equivalent fractions should lead directly on to simplifying fractions. Just as knowledge of multiples should aid children in creating equivalent fractions so knowledge of factors should aid children in simplifying fractions. The connection between multiples and factors needs to be made explicit to children. Within this, they will also need to develop an understanding of mixed fractions, e.g. $4\frac{1}{4}$, and their relationship to the improper or 'top heavy' fraction $\frac{5}{4}$.

As has been stated, having an understanding of the ordinal aspect of fractions is important in developing understanding. Therefore representations can be made of decimals and fractions using number lines in the form of 'washing lines', i.e. lines on which to hang representations.

> Place the following fractions on a number line $\frac{1}{4}$, $\frac{1}{2}$, $\frac{3}{4}$, $\frac{1}{5}$, $\frac{1}{10}$, $\frac{3}{5}$, $\frac{1}{3}$, 10%, 50%, 0.25, 0.75.

Connections need to be made to measurement. At this stage the emphasis should be supporting children working with notation. However, if they are unable to understand the concept of equivalent fractions without concrete resources then games, such as Snap, could be used pairing notation of a fraction with a geometric diagram.

Ratio and proportion

Notation for ratio relates to equivalence of fractions and the same strategy for simplifying fractions is used to simplify ratios. For example, $\frac{1}{4}$ relates to 1 : 3 in that the fraction shows one part out of four is used and the ratio shows that for every one part that is used, there are three parts that are not used.

Representations of food can emphasise this aspect of fractions.

Practical contexts make sense of ratio to children. Use of map scales or cooking activities make the mathematics relevant.

Index notation

An index number is a number which tells us how many times we must multiply another number by itself. Consider 3^2 or 4^3. Index notation is generally introduced using geometric representations and the index number is then seen as a shorthand way of recording notation of repeated

Structural apparatus or squared paper can be used to represent index numbers. Representations are most clear though when they are related to visual contexts such as area to illustrate squaring and volume for cubic notation. Equivalence in the language used needs to be emphasised. We use the term 'index' multiplication. However, it is important to be clear in explanations to children about the meaning of such numbers, i.e. that they stand for the power to which a number is multiplied or the number of times a number is multiplied by itself, i.e. 4^3 means $4 \times 4 \times 4$ and is equal to 64.

When index notation is considered with respect to the number 10, it relates to our place value system. For example, 10^0 is 1 and relates to the ones column and 10^1 is 10 and this relates to the tens column. Following this pattern, 10^2 is 100 and so on. This allows us to represent numbers that would be very cumbersome if represented in the traditional column form.

number but when verbalising notation the term 'power' is used. This is further confused by the fact that a number to the power of two is called 'squared' and a number to the power of three is called 'cubed':

3^2 'three squared'

2^3 'two cubed'

2^4 'two to the power of four'

Although there is little development of index notation beyond that associated with square and cube numbers associated with shape and measurement in the primary school, such equivalent language needs to be used to avoid children developing misconceptions later when they meet powers beyond three and standard form.

Negative numbers

Negative numbers are part of the set of integers. We refer to positive numbers just by the number names but negative numbers by a specific term 'negative one' etc. However, colloquially, these integers are often referred to as 'minus one' etc. The term minus, correctly, refers to the operation of subtraction. Whatever the number is called, there can be confusion associated with the dual use of the term meaning negative and subtract.

Use of number lines is the easiest way to represent negative numbers within a context of temperature. Familiarity will increase by listening to and watching weather forecasts, relating it to scientific topics such as 'Change of state'. Number lines with negative values introduce children to co-ordinate grids using all four quadrants that they will encounter at Key Stage 3.

Estimation

Discussion of estimation in relation to near equivalence has been discussed in Chapter 1. Children must learn to estimate in number, measurement and handling data with increasing sophistication as they are introduced to a widening range of contexts. They learn to estimate a number of objects,

Calculation

Rounding numbers helps children to calculate, e.g. 7 + 9 as 9 is nearly 10 therefore I can add 10 to 7 and then adjust the answer down by 1. Answers to problems need to be considered in the context of the question asked, e.g. the answer for deciding the number of round to the nearest 10, 100, 1 decimal place etc. and apply understanding of the real world to solving problems so that they are able to understand an equivalence between mathematical solutions and real world solutions. One of the means whereby children are able to carry out complex problems is by use of a calculator. Interpretation of a calculator solution, particularly if it involves division, can require children to round numbers of seven decimal places to gain an appropriate solution. A good understanding of place value is essential if children are going to transfer their mathematical solution to real-life solutions.

coaches for a school trip will need to be given in whole numbers.

Measurement

Although measurement is intrinsically approximate, children need suitable problems to enable them to make decisions about whether a number should be rounded up or down or be as exact as possible, e.g. paper to cover a display board, measuring growth of plants to test different growing conditions etc.

The children's learning

Self-assessment is a useful way to gauge children's learning which may be presented in a variety of forms. These may be used at all stages such as at the beginning or when returning to a topic, and at the end or as a continuing, developing process throughout the time spent on the topic. On the following page is one child's way of representing her knowledge and understanding.

Children need regular practice reading and writing numbers across the curriculum. Reading and writing the date, reading numbers on a keyboard and a calculator consolidate learning and provide assessment opportunities to determine children's learning. Collecting suitable data such as that related to linear measurement helps children to see the purpose of ordering numbers and so identify the value of the digits.

Finding opportunities to use number in practical contexts with a purpose such as playing board games, using money, solving puzzles and cooking will reinforce children's learning and provide assessment opportunities. It is also important not to limit such activities to addition and whole numbers. Games and activities can be adapted to encompass the four operations and fractional quantities. For example, Snap is useful for assessing understanding of equivalent fractions including decimals and percentages and adapting a recipe provides an opportunity to use ratio and proportion.

charley

8.4.94 Fractions
D.O.B. 9yrs um

1 half

4 quarters

eighth

$\frac{1}{4}$ $\frac{1}{2}$ $\frac{3}{4}$
1 quarter   1 half
          $\frac{2}{4}$
eighths are
smaller than quarters $8 < 4$

Fractions

I can use the inverse operation for splitting a
whole into fractions $10 \times 3 = 30$
                        $30 \div 3 = 10$
                        $\frac{1}{3}$ of $30 = 10$
I learnt how to do equivalent fractions with paper
and cutting. I found out that $\frac{2}{3} = \frac{4}{6}$ & $\frac{3}{4} = \frac{6}{8}$

0
  $\frac{1}{4}$ $\frac{1}{2}$ $\frac{3}{8}$ $\frac{3}{4}$
              $\frac{4}{8}$ $\frac{10}{16}$ $\frac{6}{8}$
I can put fractions on a
number line

I'm beginning to understand how to make
equivalent fractions by working with number not
pictures

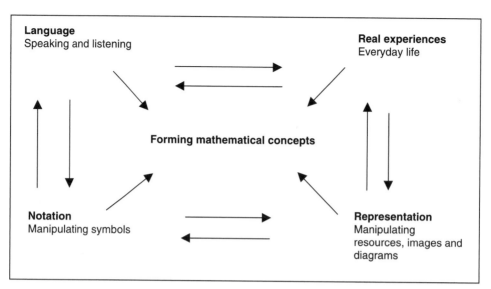

Language
Speaking and listening

Real experiences
Everyday life

Forming mathematical concepts

Notation
Manipulating symbols

Representation
Manipulating
resources, images and
diagrams

Figure 2.15

Summary

- Symbols will need to be understood in different ways by identifying the symbol with the appropriate concept. If children are not given experiences to identify appropriate concepts then they will develop **mis**conceptions.

- Our understanding of number evolves as we become aware of the increasing range of properties that numbers have. Consequently, no one aspect should dominate. Children need new experiences which will to lead to a range of connections being understood and assimilated.

- The diagram in Figure 2.15 shows the connections between language, notation, representation and real experiences from everyday life.

Calculation

Introduction

Calculation is often seen to represent mathematics. It is the term given to computation using the four operations of addition, subtraction, multiplication and division. Calculation dominates much of the numeracy taught in school, yet as a word it is rarely used in discussion. It is commonly seen as a synonym for sum, which is a word that relates solely to the operation of addition.

The teaching of calculation has dual hierarchy: (1) addition is seen as the first operation to be taught and division the last, and (2) calculations are first taught using simple whole numbers progressing through to complex fractional quantities.

Calculation cannot be seen in isolation from other aspects of number. Since the introduction of the NNS (DfEE 1999) there has been increased emphasis on using knowledge of the number system to calculate mentally. There is also significant evidence to suggest that using problem-solving as a basis for teaching calculation is more successful than teaching calculation skills first (NNS 2002). Therefore the connections between the number system, calculation and problem-solving are fundamental to being able to calculate effectively.

Understanding the equivalence *between* the operations is also significant to being able to calculate. These connections will be explored further when calculation structures are considered.

Your mathematics

In this section the following will be discussed:

- knowledge of numbers and the number system;
- the arithmetic laws which govern calculation;
- the calculation structures;
- calculation strategies;
- estimation.

Knowledge of numbers and the number system

Awareness of the properties of numbers enables calculations to be made mentally without using specific computational strategies. For example, knowing the factor pairs of 100 means that a wide range of calculations is also known such as $100 \div 20 = 5$ and $20 \times 5 = 100$. Similarly, having knowledge that we use a number system that is based on ten allows many calculations to be carried out mentally. Doing addition and subtraction with a real or visual image of a 100 square allows counting on in tens or ones. Moving backwards and forwards horizontally in ones enables simple additions and subtractions to be carried out. Moving right or counting on allows for addition and moving left or counting back allows for subtraction. Similarly, moving down vertically allows for addition in tens and moving vertically up allows for subtraction in tens. Combining both horizontal and vertical movement enables such calculations as $73 - 24$ to be worked out (from 73 move vertically up 2 rows to 53 and then backwards 4 places to 49).

> Try the above example on a 100 square. Work out some similar addition and subtraction calculations in the same way.
>
> Can you do the calculations just by visualising the square? Do you use other strategies such as verbalising what you are doing or using your fingers to count up or down in multiples of ten?
>
> Consideration of such strategies should help you support children in developing a range of calculation strategies using knowledge of the number system.

The arithmetic laws

These laws are more powerful than they may first appear. In the simplest sense, they enable us to rearrange numbers to make calculations easier. They can also make accessible knowledge of calculation facts beyond those that can be recalled immediately.

The **commutative law** relates to switching round of two numbers and applies to the operations of addition and multiplication. This can be shown using the following statements: $a + b = b + a$ and $a \times b = b \times a$.

The **associative law** concerns the order of numbers and applies to the operations of addition, subtraction and multiplication: $a + b + c = (a + b) + c = a + (b + c)$.

Using the commutative law can further extend this: as $b + c$ is equivalent to $c + b$ then $(a + c) + b = a + b + c$ as well.

The **distributive law** concerns partitioning or distributing parts of a number, treating (multiplying) them separately and then putting the parts back together again (recombining). It applies to multiplication:

$$a \times (b + c) = (a \times b) + (a \times c) \text{ or } a \times (b - c) = (a \times b) - (a \times c)$$

or

$$(a + b) \times (c + d) = (a \times c) + (a \times d) + (b \times c) + (b \times d)$$

$$\text{or } (a - b) \times (c - d) = (a \times c) - (a \times d) - (b \times c) + (b \times d)$$

This law was at one time learnt when children were introduced to the use of brackets to solve equations in algebra (usually during their secondary education). The distributive law also applies to division but it is just 'right distributive', as the division needs to be on the right side of the brackets:

$$(a + b) \div c = (a \div c) + (b \div c) \text{ and } (a - b) \div c = (a \div c) - (b \div c)$$

In other words, you can only partition the quantity (the dividend) to be divided not the number by which it is divided (the divisor).

> It can be confusing to some people when the arithmetic laws are presented algebraically. Try replacing the letters with numbers to make sense of the statements. For example, in the commutative law $7 \times 8 = 8 \times 7$ (for $a \times b = b \times a$)

Calculation structures

Each operation has a range of structures depending on the context and you need to be aware of the different structures (teaching implications will be considered later in this section). Figure 2.16 shows the inverse relationship between calculation structures.

Addition

- Aggregation – combining two or more quantities.
- Augmentation – increasing a quantity.

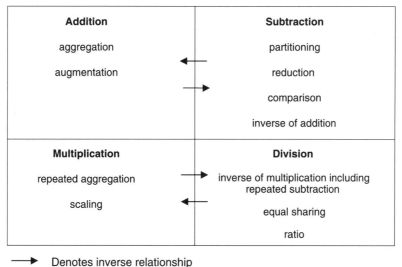

→ Denotes inverse relationship

Figure 2.16

Subtraction

- Partitioning – partitioning off a quantity.
- Reduction – reducing a quantity.
- Comparison – comparing two quantities.
- Inverse of addition or complementary addition – how much more needs to be added to a quantity.

Multiplication

- Repeated aggregation – number of amounts of a quantity.
- Scaling – increasing a quantity by a scale factor.

Division

- Equal sharing – sharing a quantity into a given number of parts.
- Inverse of multiplication – how many groups of a given number are there in a quantity?
- Ratio – scale factor by which a quantity must be increased to match another quantity.

(These structures are further exemplified in Fig. 2.18.)

Calculation strategies

In recent years there has been greater emphasis placed upon mental strategies for calculation and informal methods for written calculation. You may have learnt formal algorithms for the four operations and still use them today. Knowledge of progression and connections in key mental strategies is necessary in order to be able to teach calculation methods. Figure 2.17 shows the progression and connections in key mental strategies.

> Using the NNS Framework (DfEE 1999), track through the mental strategies and how they relate to written strategies to complete the table below (Fig. 2.17).

Estimation

Estimating answers to calculations is an important aspect of being successful in calculation. There are many equivalent ways of calculating based upon understanding of the arithmetic laws and inverse relationships of operations, some more efficient than others. Calculating an approximate answer by rounding

STRATEGY	Addition and subtraction	Multiplication and division	EXAMPLE AS A MENTAL STRATEGY	EXAMPLE AS A WRITTEN STRATEGY
Use of known facts	Use of known number facts	Use of known number facts (tables, factors, multiples		
Counting	Counting			
Number system and place value	Knowledge of number system – place value	Knowledge of number system – place value		
Reordering	Reordering			
Relationships between operations	Use of relationship between addition and subtraction	Use of relationship between multiplication and division		
Partitioning	Partitioning – and recombining	Partitioning and recombining		
	Partitioning – bridging through multiples of 10			
	Partitioning – near doubles	Doubling and halving		
	Partitioning – compensating [adding or subtracting too much and adjusting]	Partitioning and adjusting		
	Partitioning – bridging by numbers other than 10			

Figure 2.17 Progression and connections in key mental strategies

numbers up or down increases the likelihood of an answer being realistic and makes it more probable that errors can be quickly rectified.

Your teaching

Teaching that explicitly makes use of the strategies identified above will enable children to calculate effectively. Connecting appropriate language and representation to calculations is essential if children are not to develop misconceptions.

Children can, however, make false connections or over-generalisations by applying rules based on limited experiences. Below are some of the common misconceptions that children may develop based upon making false connections:

- Place value may be understood but not in the context of completing a calculation. Therefore it is important to emphasise the *quantity* involved, for example, that 32 is *thirty and two* not just 3 in the tens column and 2 in the ones.

- Addition is commutative but subtraction is *not* commutative, although subtraction is the inverse operation of addition (subtraction 'undoes' addition and vice versa).

- Multiplication is commutative but division is *not* commutative, although division is the inverse operation of multiplication (division 'undoes' multiplication and vice versa).

- Confusion can arise over the greater number of subtraction structures than addition structures, particularly in relation to 'take away' (partitioning or reduction structure) and 'difference between' (comparison structure) as both types are represented by the same mathematical operation.

- Too great a stress on multiplication is seen as repeated addition (aggregation) and not scaling so it does not fit the context of a problem.

- Estimation is seen as guessing rather than as a useful tool to check calculation.

- The equals sign being used both to show an instruction to perform a calculation as in 4 + 5 = or as representing equivalence. This is particularly important in algebra: 8 + ? = 12 which can be solved by the inverse of addition structure – what must I add to 8 to make 12?

- Confusion by some children between the signs + and ÷ if not written clearly.

Research has shown that most misconceptions are widely shared (NNS 2002) For example, if 2 squared equals 4, then 3 squared must be 6, arising from the fact that in the case of 2 squared the effect of the operations + and × is the same. Therefore teaching should make explicit possible misconceptions and use them as a point of discussion. Two of the ways that misconceptions can be exposed and rectified might be careful choice of teaching examples and probing questioning, discussed further in the next chapter.

These false connections need to be identified at the same time as making valid connections. Figure 2.18 identifies calculation structures and related notation, language, representation and possible contexts.

> Consider the everyday calculation activities that children encounter and how they relate to each structure. For example, although division is the last operation children are introduced to, it is often the one they use in practical situations, e.g. sharing food and toys. Similarly, although subtraction is frequently referred to as 'take away', everyday contexts involve reduction rather than partitioning, e.g. giving marbles away, spending pocket money and difference.

The context introduced to children should match the strategy being taught. Similarly, it is important to match language to the correct strategy. Representation needs to match the calculation structure. Some representations such as bricks and counters can match a range of structures, but representations such as number lines are useful for augmentation and reduction but not for aggregation and partitioning.

The children's learning

Children's understanding of calculation cannot be assessed by examples of completed 'sums'. They need to be able to identify a range of calculation strategies and make decisions about the most effective strategy to use based on the context and the numbers involved. Below are examples of how a child at the beginning of Year 5 approached a range of calculations.

Summary

- A secure knowledge of numbers and the number system, and the arithmetic laws enables children to carry out a range of calculations mentally.
- Teaching the skills of calculation is more likely to be successful if contextualised.
- The interrelationship of the four operations can help children make valid and false connections.
- Both valid and false connections need to be made explicit to children.
- Structures within each operation are not always equivalent so care needs to be taken in matching the correct language, notation and representation to each structure.

Structure	Notation	Language	Contexts	Representation
Addition structures				
Aggregation	3 + 4	Add, and, altogether, plus, sum of, total 3 add 4	Combining two or more sets into one set as in money and measures. How much have I spent/drunk/travelled altogether?	Everyday objects, bricks, counters and 2D images of them leading on to children making their own representations and/or mental images.
Augmentation	3 + 4	Count on, increase by, more than 4 more than 3	Measures, particularly money.	Everyday objects, bricks, counters and 2D images of them leading on to children making their own representations and/or mental images. Number grids and lines.
Subtraction structures				
Partitioning	12 – 5	Take away, subtract, minus 12 take away 5	Working out quantity left when part taken away, particularly in money and measurement contexts.	Everyday objects, bricks, counters and 2D images of them leading on to children making their own representations and/or mental images.
Reduction	12 – 5	Count back, decrease by, less than 5 less than 12	Money, temperature.	Everyday objects, bricks, counters and 2D images of them leading on to children making their own representations and/or mental images. Number grids and lines.
Comparison	12 – 5 Some of the language used can cause confusion as more is associated with addition.	Difference between, how much bigger/smaller? How much/many more? What is the difference between 5 and 12? How many more is 12 than 5? How many less is 5 than 12?	Comparing any quantity but particularly measurement.	Number rods and 2D images of them leading on to children making their own representations and/or mental images.

Inverse of addition or complementary addition	12 – 5 As the language associated with this structure relates to addition – more and add – children may record addition notation or enter the wrong calculation on a calculator. Notation can also be in the form of 5 + ? = 12	How many/much more? How many more is 12 than 5? What must I add to 5 to make 12?	Money, measurement particularly if competitive as in sport.	Number lines leading on to children making their own representations and/or mental images.
Multiplication structures				
Repeated aggregation	3 + 3 + 3 + 3	Sets of, lots of, groups of 4 sets of 3	Measurement.	Sets of everyday objects, bricks, counters and 2D images of them leading on to children making their own representations and/or mental images. Arrays are a good method of representing the commutative aspect of multiplication and the idea that multiplication is repeated aggregation. It relates well to both repeated aggregation and scaling structures. * * * *　　3 sets of 4 and 4 sets of 3 * * * *　　depending whether viewed * * * *　　horizontally or vertically.
Scaling	4 × 3	How many times as much/many? 4 times 3	Scale models, maps.	Number rods and representations of them are also useful for the scaling structure leading on to children making their own representations and/or mental images.

Structure	Notation	Language	Contexts	Representation
Division structures				
Equal sharing	10 ÷ 5 = 2 10 sweets shared between 2 people.	Share/divide between Share 10 sweets between 5 people – how many does each person get?	Classroom contexts that involve dividing quantity equally between people of given number.	Everyday objects, bricks, counters and 2D images of them leading on to children making their own representations and/or mental images.
Inverse of multiplication	10 ÷ 2 = 5 How many groups of 2 are there in 10? The notation is the reverse of the language used and like the inverse of addition structure children may record incorrect notation or enter the wrong calculation on a calculator.	How many groups/sets How many groups of 2 are there in 10? (relates to repeated addition and subtraction)	Classroom contexts that involve formation of groups of given number from a quantity.	Everyday objects, bricks, counters and 2D images of them leading on to children making their own representations and/or mental images. Arrays as stated above are particularly useful for representing this structure.
Ratio	10 ÷ 5 = 2 Using the term times can confuse children with the notation of multiplication.	How many times older/faster/longer etc.? I am 10 and my brother is 5. How many times older than my brother am I?	Measurement, particularly distance, but care must be taken to find contexts that are meaningful. Knowing how many times something is older/longer/shorter etc. is not usually relevant to primary age children.	Number rods leading on to children making their own representations and/or mental images.

Figure 2.18

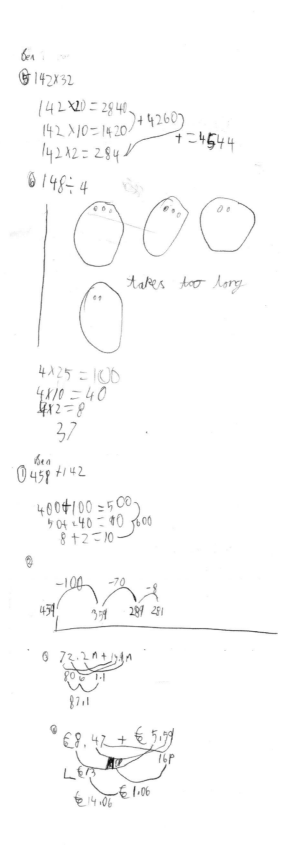

Ben

ⓐ 142×32

142×20 = 2840
142×10 = 1420 } +4260
142×2 = 284 } + = 4544

ⓑ 148÷4

takes too long

4×25 = 100
4×10 = 40
4×2 = 8
37

Ben

① 458 +142

400+100 = 500
50+40 = 90 } 600
8 +2 = 10

②

−100   −70   −8
459   359   289 281

③ 72.2m + 14.9m
80.6   1.1
87.1

④ €8.47 + €5.59
€13   16p
€14.06   €1.06

Solving numeric problems

Introduction

Teachers are frequently being urged to teach problem-solving as it is 'at the heart of mathematics' (Cockcroft 1982: 249) but with the frequent 'back to basics' calls, teachers tend to concentrate more on teaching how to *do* mathematics, rather than how to *use* it. Nevertheless, the reality is that for the majority of future adults, their use of mathematics will be to resolve problems, be they as small as calculating the right change at the shop or as large as the calculation of the best aerodynamic shape for a new aeroplane.

But what is problem-solving in mathematics? The two examples above give an indication of the range of problems, but a definition here would be useful to place it in the context of classroom mathematics. In the broadest terms, a problem is a question or matter that has been raised for examination, consideration and/or solution. Furthermore, it is worth bearing in mind that mathematically a problem is something to be resolved whereas a theorem is something to be proved.

Mathematics is perceived by many to be a subject in which you are either right or wrong, and that being right is only achieved by the few who are good at mathematics. An extension of this belief is that if you can apply the appropriate formulae and algorithms then you are good at mathematics. This image of a mathematician denies the reality of mathematics as a highly creative field in which flexibility and laterality of thought are core attributes for success. Making connections is the key to successful problem-solving. Mathematical problems may have a direct, real-life application, which provides a context and relevance to the children. But they may also have intrinsic value. Pleasure in problem-solving for its own sake should form a part of all children's cognitive development and not be regarded as the domain of a few unusual children.

Current models for teaching mathematics at primary school level endeavour to address flexible approaches to mathematics by encouraging the teaching of strategies rather than procedures, although it could be argued that once a strategy has been taught as the 'best' way to approach a particular type of problem, it then becomes a procedure, subject to the constraints and opportunities for errors and misconceptions to occur when procedures are followed without question. However, by giving children access to a range of approaches and by helping them to make decisions about choices, the teacher is enabling children to become more effective problem-solvers.

Your mathematics

Algebra

Algebra is not explored extensively in this book but this is not to trivialise the power and importance of the subject. Here, we consider it within its role in problem-solving. Within several of these strategies, the organisation of any interim information, whether formally or informally, is important to enable progress to be tracked through both specific and general statements. The representation that lends itself to this, algebra and algebraic notation, is a generally understood system that provides a common ground for effective communication. In problem-solving terms, all this means in its simplest form is that you used symbols to represent what you did not know and wanted to find out.

One use of algebra in problem-solving is that of expressing a rule in a number pattern. The number pattern is often generated as a result of a problem-solving activity and is part of the organisation of information that can lead to a solution to the problem. As can be seen, the rule is a development from the number machines of early mathematics.

Pattern (n)	Rule	Outcome (y)	In this example, it is clear that 1 has been added to the
1		2	starting number to give the outcome. This can be
2		3	expressed algebraically as:
3	+1	4	$y = n + 1$
4		5	This means that for any value of n, we can determine
5		6	a value for y.

Pattern (n)	Rule	Outcome (y)	In this example, it is clear that the starting number has
1		2	been doubled to give the outcome. This can be
2		4	expressed algebraically as:
3	x2	6	$y = 2n$
4		8	This means that for any value of n, we can determine
5		10	a value for y.

(n)	rule	step	rule	(y)	In this example, the outcome goes up in 2s. This
1		2		3	multiplication gives the clue to the first part of the rule.
2		4		5	After applying this, it can then be decided what needs
3	x2	6	+1	7	to be done to achieve the outcome – in this case, +1.
4		8		9	The whole rule can then be expressed algebraically
5		10		11	as:
					$y = 2n + 1$

Figure 2.19

There are much more complex algebraic rules or generalisations that arise out of different number patterns, but these simple steps give an indication of the relevance to primary mathematics.

Models

One way to bring all of these elements together is by using models to support the problem-solving process. These have been around for many years and have been adjusted to suit the situation in which they are being used. An Internet search will bring up many hundreds of references to models in a variety of formats – some give flow diagrams, some frames, some stages, some cycles, some simple, some complex. Three fairly old and typical models are outlined in Figure 2.20.

Polya (1945 and 1962)
This is generally accepted to be the first model based on classroom practice:
- Understand the problem
- Devise a plan
- Carry out the plan
- Look back

Dewey (1910)
This is a model based on the scientific process:
- Define the problem
- Suggest possible solutions and identify alternatives
- Reason about the solutions and implement
- Test and prove

Wallis (1926)
This model is based on the creative process:
- Problem formulation and information gathering
- Incubation – allowing the unconscious to work on it
- Illumination – working to gain insight
- Verification – testing for accuracy

Figure 2.20

Consider yourself as a problem-solver. You may or may not be confident in your mathematical problem-solving abilities so, initially, use the general definitions for problems considered at the beginning of this section and think how you attempt to solve a problem. You will have met definitions of several cognitive styles, but the grasshopper/inchworm styles (Bath *et al.* cited in Chinn and Ashcroft 1998) are useful mental images at this stage as they offer views of either end of the range of cognitive styles (the inchworm focuses on the parts and details and works in ordered, forward steps on a single method while the grasshopper considers an overview and works with several methods, both backwards and forwards). It may help to think of a problem that you are currently pondering.

How do you tackle a problem? Do you have a grasshopper approach or that of an inchworm? How easily do you make connections? Are these close or distant connections?

What sorts of representations and notations do you use to help support your progress?

How do you organise your work?

Which of these three models appeals to you most? How are they similar and how are they different? What is your first impression?

Now try to apply each of them to a school-based problem, such as working out the timings for a school trip or budgeting for resources in your subject area.

> Which one works for you now?
> How many connections did you make?

Although the examination of problem-solving above has been in a general context, mathematical problems require similar approaches in order to reach a solution regardless of the mathematics required.

Try one of the examples in Figure 2.21 using the model you seem to prefer.

On the first day of term, every member of a staff of 12 shakes hands with every other member of staff. How many handshakes will there be? How many handshakes will there be if each child in a class of 30 shakes hands with every other child in the class? How many handshakes would there be for the whole school (of any number)?

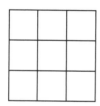 How many squares are there in this figure?
How many would there be in a 4 x 4 square?
How many would there be in a 12 x 12 square?
How many would there be in a 3 x 4 oblong?
How many would there be in a 3 x 5 oblong?
How many would there be in a 12 x 15 oblong?

Imagine an immense tornado picked up the great pyramid of Giza and transported it and then dropped it on top of your school. Supposing it remained intact, where could the four corners of the base be?

Figure 2.21

> For any of the problems above, did you use algebra to explain any of the rules you found?

There are, of course, many mathematical problems with a wide range of complexity and mathematical requirements. But for all, an approach strategy is required and to succeed, that approach needs to be the most appropriate for both the problem and the problem-solver.

Do a general web search for models and problems and see what you come up with. Try some mathematics and/or teaching websites. What do they offer that you could use or adapt in your classroom?

What models do you already have in your school – in files, commercial schemes etc.?

Make a collection of everything you can find and organise it into learning styles, usefulness in the classroom, adaptability, nature of support or any alternative ways you might find useful.

Your teaching

One of the skills of teaching effectively is the decisions you make about how much to tell the children and how much they should find out for themselves. In the previous section, you examined yourself as a problem-solver and your experience, attitude and confidence in this area will have a bearing on your approach to teaching. As always, however, thorough planning can provide you with the opportunity to rehearse much of the expected progression that you and the children will make through the lesson.

As with much of mathematics teaching, the learning of problem-solving skills is developmental and the choice and presentation of problems needs to reflect this. Simple, one-stage problems should precede two-stage problems. Within two-stage problems, information given in the required order for solving is cognitively simpler than if the information is mixed, not necessarily in any order. In addition to this, the size and type of numbers chosen will also affect the child's perception of the difficulty of the problem.

Can you list the categories of problems you will need to teach progressively in terms of their complexity, from simple one-stage problems right through to complex, multi-stage problems that include redundant information?

One marble costs 20p. How much do 3 marbles cost?

Using this problem as a starting point, develop it into increasingly complex problems, one or more for each category you defined above. How have you used choice of number to extend the possibilities?

Representation and notation

Jottings

Recent work on the use of jottings by the NNS (1999) has highlighted the valuable role these play in supporting children's progress through their mathematical reasoning. Often idiosyncratic, jottings bridge the gap between holding everything in the head and the formalised use of procedural recording. When coupled with verbalised explanations, these individualised representations not only show what the child has done but also serve to enhance their articulation of their thoughts and so contribute to their understanding and progress.

The National Curriculum requires that children 'organise work and refine ways of recording' and 'use notation diagrams and symbols correctly within a given problem'. Problems are solved when an appropriate solution is found from the various strategies employed during the work. While jottings support this, organised representations, using relevant notation, will not only inform the problem-solver but also any interested audience, both immediately and on return to the work, for whatever purpose. The skill of the teacher is to teach children how to use their own individual thinking styles (e.g. inchworm or grasshopper) to be successful in problem-solving.

Problem-solving skills

You can teach skills that will help to support the children's decision-making and choice of strategies. Some of the general strategies that can be used for problem-solving are:

- clue words;
- diagrams;
- models;
- breaking down the problem;
- searching for patterns;
- looking for familiar parts;
- checking;
- reasoning.

Clue words

Searching for clue or key words within the wording of the problem can give indications of the type of calculation needed. Development of mathematical vocabulary is an integral part of mathematics teaching, and the four basic operations each have a number of words that reflect their meaning.

It is worth bearing in mind, however, that many of these words have other meanings that may be the same, different or similar to their mathematical meaning (as discussed in Ch. 1). As the interpretation of clue words is a skill that is useful in problem-solving, when posing problems to the children for solving, you need to decide whether you want to use the language as a clue or whether you want to include possibly misleading words as a challenge to their problem-solving development. For example, while 'difference' can mean a subtraction operation through comparison is required (as in 'What is the difference between the ages of the oldest and the youngest child in the school?'), it can also require another sort

As a reminder, fill in as many synonyms as you can remember (see pages 41–42 for help):

+	−
×	÷

Figure 2.22

of comparison (as in 'What is the difference between an equilateral triangle and an isosceles triangle?').

Take some of the problems you devised earlier based on the 20p marble. How can you reword them so that the operation required is obvious from the use of clue words, and then again so that the child would have to look beyond the clue words as they may be misleading?

Diagrams and models

Diagrams and models help to break down the problem into parts. For many children, the problem as a whole can be overwhelming, whether presented orally to be received aurally or in a written format. They cannot fathom out where and how to get started and so can lose confidence in their ability to make any progress. By teaching them the skills of simplifying and separating, they can develop the strategies with which they can clarify the picture and tackle the problem.

Again take some of the more complex problems that resulted from the simple marble problem above. How many different ways can you teach the children to break down the problems in order to clarify what needs to be done? What different representations have you considered? What differences would you have to take into account between teaching the children to listen to the problem and teaching them to read it?

Searching for patterns

Searching for patterns is one of the keys to effective problem-solving. If children can see patterns developing, they can start to make predictions and then test out those predictions with further evidence. Children who work in a predominantly random manner will have much more difficulty seeing patterns emerging. Once the problem has been broken down and the child can identify an approach that will lead to a solution, the role of the teacher is to teach strategies for organising the progression of the work so that children have the opportunity to decide whether or not there is a pattern. This is not to suggest that at the start of an endeavour to solve a problem, we should expect the children to organise their work immediately. Often, the most appropriate means of organisation starts to present itself once we have a few bits of information, jotted down, which we can then set out in a useful way. One of the hardest things for children in problem-solving is the need to record their thought processes at a time when they are jumping mentally from one possibility to another. We should allow this trial time and acknowledge its value as an exploratory period that encourages drawing on pre-existing and wide-ranging knowledge and understanding.

> When you looked at yourself as a problem-solver earlier in the chapter, how organised were you? How many ways of organising findings have you taught in the past?

Children learn from each other and your role, as a teacher, is not only to provide models of organisation for them, depending on their differentiated needs, but also to use peer support and discussion so that the children can develop awareness of appropriateness and suitability of recording for the task.

> When you worked with children on solving problems, which strategies did you offer to help them organise their work? Have you found that the children devised their own organisational strategies? If so, what did you observe?

Once the work has an organisational structure then patterns become more evident; at this point, gaps in information become apparent which then can be resolved. The representation and notation at this stage will vary greatly according to the ability and stage of development of the children and the nature of the problem. In many situations, communication of interim findings and solutions to the problem may well be required in word form, either spoken or written.

> Return to your chart of increasingly complex problems: to which would you ask the children to respond verbally and to which would you require a written response using narrative form? How would you use this to teach the correct mathematical use of vocabulary?

As already mentioned, appropriate mathematical notation is an efficient system of communication, and for problem-solving this will probably mean something from simple number sentences through equations to algebraic representation. None of these, however, should be taught to the exclusion of the language that is more naturally understood by the children. The basic problem about the marbles can be used to illustrate this (Fig. 2.23).

Problem	Language	Number sentence	Answer
One marble costs 20p. How much do 3 marbles cost?	3 lots of 20p can be 20p add 20p add 20p	20p + 20p + 20p = ?	
	or 3 lots of 20p	20p × 3 = ?	60p
	or 20p, 3 times	20p × 3 = ?	
	or double 20p and add 20p	20p × 2 + 20p = ?	

Figure 2.23

As the children become more proficient problem-solvers, you may ask for deductions to be made from patterns using algebraic representation as the most suitable form of notation. You need to plan with care how you will introduce to the children the nature and choice of symbols. It can be seen from Figure 2.23 that the letter 'p' is used to represent a penny, not an unknown. Letters are used in all areas of mathematics to represent such things as units of measure; to then teach that they are to be used for a different purpose has potential for confusion.

How many letters can you think of that are used in ordinary number sentences?

Early number work introduces the use of symbols to represent unknowns and so even young children become accustomed to their use (see Fig. 2.24).

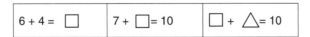

Figure 2.24

What other early number work forms the basis for algebra?

A decision to teach the use of letters to only some children in the class, for differentiation purposes, does not necessarily place restrictions on the problem to be solved – only on the way in which the solution is communicated. The pattern below (Fig. 2.25) could be taken to be the organised findings from this problem-solving challenge.

These are the first three in a pattern of triangles made with matchsticks.
How many matchsticks will you need for the 5th pattern (with 5 triangles)?
How many matchsticks for 20 triangles?
How many matchsticks for any number of triangles?

Number of triangles (n)	Number of matchsticks (y)	Narrative generalisation	Algebraic generalisation
1	3.	Double the number of triangles and then add 1 to get the number of matchsticks.	$y = 2n + 1$
2	5		
3	7		
4	9		
5	11		

Figure 2.25

Think of some other problem-solving activities that have resulted in a pattern of numbers. Can you represent the generalisation verbally, pictorially, narratively and algebraically? What factors would contribute to how you decide which representation you would teach at any one time? How does the nature of the representation contribute to the level of mathematical achievement?

The children's learning

The way in which the nature of the representation contributes to the level of mathematical achievement is one of the key questions to be addressed when determining the effectiveness of your teaching. The language of mathematics and the way in which it is communicated through representation and notation is an important part of how we assess children's learning. In particular, problem-solving requires children to interpret the problem given before they can solve it and then to present not only their answer, but also the way in which they reached that answer. Yet it is reasonable to argue that language development is not a measure of mathematical cognitive development. It is therefore sometimes difficult to assess the progress in mathematical problem-solving for those children whose language development may inhibit them from demonstrating their mathematical ability. Sometimes, for these children, the symbols of mathematics notation remove ambiguity so enabling them to achieve clarity in their understanding of the requirements and also in their expression of the solution. But, it could then be argued that this is also removing the interpretation and analysis of a problem's requirements, so limiting a large part of the nature of problem-solving and reducing it to little more than calculations. So the argument goes round in a circle. As discussed at the start of this section, however, the ability to apply mathematics to the solving of problems is what mathematics is all about and therefore as teachers you need to assess children's learning in this area. The summative assessments that children undertake endeavour to assess problem-solving through a variety of means of communication.

Look at some recent, externally produced, summative assessment papers from both Key Stages 1 and 2. Consider some of the problems the children are asked to solve. In which ways have the children been able to represent their solutions? How have the setters of the papers accounted for those children with delayed literacy development?
Does this allow these children to give a true picture of themselves as mathematical problem-solvers?

Of course, the summative assessments are only one way in which to evaluate the effectiveness of our teaching through the children's learning. On a daily basis in our classroom we engage in formative assessment which we organise formally, through our lesson planning, or informally through our observations from working with the children. In this way, we can form an all-round picture of each child's problem-solving ability, including the language question, as we have opportunities to assess both the effect when language is a focus and when it is not. Assessing a part of the problem-solving process is not only useful for analysis of future teaching and learning requirements but is also feasible from a practical perspective when management of the class has to be considered. Some of the parts of the problem-solving process that you would intend taking place within mathematical problem-solving will include:

- interpreting given information;
- breaking down problems into component parts;
- determining order of events;
- transference of previously learned mathematical knowledge, skills and understanding;
- application of specific calculation skills;
- use of informal notes and jottings;
- choice of resources to support progress through the problem-solving process;

- ordering and organisation of derived facts and information;
- review and assessment of progress;
- interpretation of derived facts and information;
- representation of processes and solutions in an appropriate manner;
- recursive rules and generalisations expressed aurally, narratively and/or algebraically.

Can you think of others? Consider some of the problems already used in this chapter with a view to assessing one or more of the above. How would you assess a child in order to find out how s/he has progressed within one or more of these aspects?

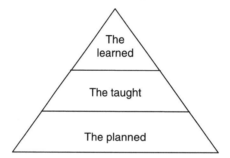

Figure 2.26

At a generic level the curriculum can be considered on three levels, as shown in Fig. 2.26. Within mathematics this is sometimes easy to track, but in problem-solving it may be quite difficult to follow the progress of the children from what you have planned to what they have learned. The ongoing system of evaluation and assessment that we undertake as teachers enables us to determine how much of what we planned to teach has been learned. A spirally based curriculum builds on this to provide the opportunities to teach more effectively through learning provided via a range of problems that repeatedly address specifically targeted aspects set in different contexts. Much of the intended learning in problem-solving is difficult to quantify and therefore is better judged by the evidence of progress.

How would progress in any one area be judged against previous progress in the same area?

Choose a school year that you are currently teaching or have taught recently and consider one or more of the learning intentions noted above. How would you plan a spirally based progression for a year group in that area, including assessment?

Summary

- Problem-solving crosses all areas of mathematics and the rest of the curriculum.

- Way and means of solving problems need to be taught in order to provide children with the opportunities to develop and refine their instinctive abilities. In order to be able to do that, teachers need to feel confident about their own problem-solving strategies.

- Language is the medium through which we access the requirements of any problem and therefore teachers need to be aware of the limitations this can place on the progression of learning for some children.

- In conjunction with this, there are many ways to communicate both the requirements of a problem and the means by which a solution has been achieved, including orally, written narrative form and both standard/non-standard mathematical representation and notation.

- In most cases, success in problem-solving is evident by the outcome, but determination of the effectiveness of learning about the different strands of problem-solving sometimes needs more structured and planned assessment.

CHAPTER 3

Shape, space and measures

SOME KEY CONNECTIONS WITHIN AND ACROSS ATTAINMENT TARGETS

- Patterns in number and shape.
- Properties of number and shape.
- Conservation in measurement and representation of numbers.
- Transformation in shape and numbers through equivalence.
- Proof in shape and number.
- Transitivity in measures and number.
- 2D and 3D shapes.
- Abstraction of 2D representations and reality of 3D representation.

Using and applying shape, space and measures

Introduction

There are many connections from using and applying shape, space and measures to other aspects of mathematics. Understanding the concept of pattern is more accessible visually than through notation. Similarly mathematical reasoning which involves communicating mathematically and explaining, making generalisations and proof is often more easily understood through shape and space than number as it provides immediate opportunities to accommodate a range of learning styles. Children can move shapes around, draw patterns, look at their own visual representations as well as those offered to them, and become involved with investigational activities working individually or in groups. A question using numbers, such as why an even number can be written as the sum of two odd numbers, may have to go through an additional stage of developing representations to match the notation. It is interesting to note that rarely would a teacher start work on shape by just talking about it and not use resources, as sometimes can be the case with number work.

Using and applying measurement has a clear but tenuous link with shape and space. Shape, space and measures relate to geometric problems. If considering application of measurement there is a tendency to relate it only to the dimensions of shape and space that often leads on to everyday life projects, e.g. calculating the costs of activities such as redecorating a bedroom or packaging solutions. Children, however, need to consider the concept of measurement and its connection to shape and space, not merely how to calculate working with the dimensions of shape and space. Why do we use different units of measurement? What is the equivalence between these different units? How appropriate are those units to problems that need to be solved?

Your mathematics

You may find that you have forgotten much of what you learnt at school about shape, space and measures simply because you are not using and applying it to everyday life or other areas of mathematics. It is difficult to define what you need to know in order to help children use and apply shape, space and measures. Knowledge and understanding of shape, space and measures gives teachers the confidence they need to structure children's learning so that they have the opportunities to solve problems, communicate and reason. Taking this perspective, teachers have to be secure in the knowledge of properties of shapes and units of measurement.

> Look in *Mathematical Vocabulary* (NNS 1999) at the vocabulary used in Year 6 for shape, space and measures. Check your understanding of the terminology with a mathematical dictionary.

Reasoning and proof

In addition to knowledge of properties of shapes and units of measurement, teachers need a clear understanding of mathematical reasoning and proof. This enables them to make effective connections between shape, space and measures and other aspects of mathematics.

Primary children are expected to develop their assumptions or conjectures about specific examples to explore whether they can make generalisations. They do not, however, need to develop generalisations to formal proof – rather, they need to develop explanations to show why their generalisations are valid. Nevertheless, teachers need to be aware of the sorts of examples that may occur at primary level and to what types of proof they relate:

- Counter-example – disprove by finding an example that does not match a conjecture.
- Deduction – proof deduced by a logical chain of reasoning starting with what is known.

- Induction – proof by looking at specific examples and consideration of whether it is true for all examples.
- Exhaustion – finding all possible solutions by checking all possibilities, e.g. that there are only 11 unique nets of closed cubes. This exhaustion can be determined through the systematic recording of all possible combinations of arrangements of six squares that also can be formed into closed cubes.

> Can you think of a proof by exhaustion relating to number? Remember you must 'exhaust' all possibilities.

Your teaching

Expectations in Mathematics attainment target 1 (Ma 1) related to mathematical reasoning and proof are identified in the National Curriculum at Key Stage 1 as the development of skills such as:

Understand a general statement and investigate whether particular cases match it.
Use mathematical communication and explanation skills.
Explain their methods of reasoning when solving problems.

And at Key Stage 2:

Explain and communicate mathematically.
Make connections in mathematics.
Use checking procedures.
Search for pattern.
Use mathematical reasoning.

The skills required of children cannot be learnt quickly but are acquired over a period of time. Structured teaching situations are needed to allow children to 'come to know' rather than be told. There is no simple way of teaching children to communicate, generalise, explain and reason. Teaching, however, should include the following elements.

Making connections

Classification, conservation, equivalence and transitivity are not exclusive to shape, space and measures and can be connected to other mathematical topics.

Classification in shapes, space and measures

Properties of shapes, e.g. categorising shapes according to properties – quadrilateral, triangles, faces, edges and vertices of 3D shapes.

Could be connected to:

Properties of numbers, e.g. categorising numbers according to property – odd, prime, squares, factors and triangular numbers.

Comparison and ordering – e.g. numbers greater than 50.

Conservation in shapes, space and measures

Length – two objects remain the same length even if the orientation of one is changed.

Mass – altering the shape of two equal pieces of plasticine that have been balanced does not alter the mass.

Capacity – pouring the liquid from one container to another of different shape does not alter the amount of liquid.

Area – rearranging parts of a 2D shape (with no overlaps) does not alter the area.

Shape – angles remain the same when a shape is transformed in some way, e.g. enlarged.

Could be connected to:

Number – arrays of counters – understanding that the arrangement of counters does not alter the number of counters (as shown in Fig 3.1).

Figure 3.1

Equivalence in shape, space and measures

Shape – when shapes are transformed by being translated, rotated or reflected they produce equivalent shapes. The term 'congruent' is used to describe equivalence between shapes.

Measures – e.g. 100 centimetres = 1 metre and approximately 2.5 centimetres ≈ 1 inch.

Could be connected to:

Numbers represented in different forms, e.g. $^1/_2$ of 6, $^2/_4$ of 6, 0.5 of 6 and 50% of 6; 278 = 200 + 70 + 8

$70 = 8 \times 8 + 6$

$2^2 \times 3^2 = 36$

Notation in equivalent forms, e.g. ÷ and / and the same form of notation representing different concepts: $^1/_4$ can mean of a whole, $^1/_4$ of a number, 1 ÷ 4, $^1/_4$ on a number line, ratio, scale factor etc.

Operations, e.g. inverse relationships $3 \times 7 = 21$ and $21 \div 7 = 3$ or $21 \div 3 = 7$.

Transitivity in shape, space and measures

Measurement – transitivity can be described for some situations where, if two measurements A and B have a relationship, and B and another measurement C have the same relationship, then A and C will also have the same relationship. For example, if A is less than B and B is less than C, then A will be less than C. Care must be taken, however, when considering the nature of this relationship, especially once the nature of the relationship is specified. For example, if we can say that 2 is half of 4 and also that 1 is half of 2, we cannot say that 1 is therefore half of 4.

Could be connected to:

Number – e.g. if 3 is a factor of 6 and 6 is a factor of 12, then 3 is a factor of 12. Connections must also be made explicit in language, notation and representation used. This has been identified in the following sections of this chapter concerning properties of shape, position and movement, and measures.

Misconceptions

Specific misconceptions are identified in subsequent sections related to understanding properties of shape, position and movement, and measures. Those related to using and applying shape, space and measures often connect to problem-solving and language.

Problem-solving

Children need to develop a range of problem-solving strategies. Teaching needs to identify connections between a strategy used in number work that could be used in shape, space and measures work (see Ch. 2, 'Solving numeric problems' for problem-solving strategies).

Language

Adults as well as children can use language inappropriately or too generally. Making connections between the everyday world and school mathematics is generally considered helpful so that children can make sense of what they are doing and so make use and application easier. But, particularly when working with shape, confusion can arise because of the inaccurate use of terminology to describe shape, e.g. a 'round' for a circle or a sphere or 'diamond' to describe a rhombus. Making connections to the everyday use of language associated with shape cannot be ignored but identification of these ambiguous connections has to be made explicit in teaching. Teachers need to provide models, resources and accurate mathematical language to enable children to communicate correctly and develop verbal explanation skills when justifying decisions. It is particularly important to model ways to interpret problems by identifying key words, identifying the number of criteria or constraints and what strategies children could use to investigate the problem and check their results.

> Identify key words and any criteria or constraints in the problem below. What strategies could you use to solve the problem?
>
> Can you identify a pattern so that you can calculate the number of faces, edges or vertices of a 3D shape if you know two of the three properties?

Taking a constructivist viewpoint, children create their own conceptual structures. The more connections children make between the various aspects of their learning the more likely they are to apply what they have learnt and so grasp new concepts. Therefore questions that encourage children to make these connections are an important element of taking the teaching process forward, e.g.:

Can you see a pattern?
What shapes shall we use next?
That's interesting – can you tell me why . . .?
What if . . .?

> The NNS probing questions in *Using Assess and Review Lessons* (DfES 2001) for shape, space and measures are provided to support and extend existing practice. How could you develop your questioning skills using this material?

Use of resources

Allowing children to choose the resources they will use or select from a range provided by you will again enhance their ability to apply their knowledge to new situations. For example, if asked to design packaging they will need to make connections and apply their knowledge of capacity, factors of numbers and area of nets of shapes. To work on this problem, they may choose just to make sketches, a 3D model or use 3D bricks. Their choice of resources will depend not just on their mathematical ability but also on their preferred style of learning. Some will prefer a practical, kinaesthetic approach that allows them to try to improve through experimentation while others will prefer to visualise shapes and the possibilities and then represent these diagrammatically, before starting to make the model. Whatever their preferred style, some children will want faster solutions and others will take a varied approach in order to check results. Also, children may prefer/be successful working alone whereas some may need to work with others to articulate their ideas and develop explanation skills.

The children's learning

Junk modelling is a useful activity to assess children's understanding of shape, space and measures and can be linked to other curriculum areas such as geography. For example, at Key Stage 1 children could work in small groups to make a model of their school or locality from a range of packaging. Apart from extending geographical enquiry and skills, children would have the opportunity to demonstrate problem-solving skills such as selecting equipment and materials, trying different approaches to problems as well as developing communication and explanation skills (ideas developed from *The National Curriculum: Handbook for Primary Teachers in England* (DfEE/QCA 1999)).

> Identify an activity related to another curriculum area that would encourage children to apply their knowledge and understanding of shapes, space and measures. Think about grouping the children, those who would need support with fine motor skills such as cutting, resources that you would need to supply including adult support and name the objectives that you want children to meet by carrying out the task.

Summary

- Teaching needs to model language and strategies for solving problems.

- Appropriate connections need to be made to calculation skills to solve geometric questions and vice versa.

- The classroom environment needs to be set up so children can choose resources and work independently or with others.

Understanding properties of shape

Introduction

Shape is a mathematics topic with a fairly distinct vocabulary that we rarely refer to in everyday life, yet shape is all around us. For example, a cube is a familiar word that is used in everyday conversation but a cuboid is not. Also words are used inaccurately to describe shape such as 'round' for a circle and 2D names for 3D shapes (rectangle for cuboid). Equivalence is a concept that comes in various guises in shape – symmetry, similarity and congruence. Symmetry involves consideration of equivalence and balance *within* a shape whereas similarity and congruence involve equivalence *between* two or more shapes. Although work with shape has a strong visual element, many people are not always able to classify shapes as the visual representation can be distorted by their mental image of a shape that has evolved from their experiences. For example, when a group of students was asked to draw a triangle, they generally drew an isosceles or equilateral triangle 'sitting' on one side. This is because of the way that triangles are often represented to us as children. Other less familiar triangles presented to the students along with a range of plane shapes were not immediately seen as triangles. The need to return to a definition of a shape based upon numerically based properties became evident. Relating visual representation to language and notation will be explored further in this section.

Your mathematics

Subject knowledge to teach properties of shape can be divided into three broad areas: 2D shapes, 3D shapes and constructions including nets of shapes. You may find that you have forgotten much of the terminology associated with shape. The specific language used enables shapes to be classified into categories and the process of classification helps us make sense of our experiences. The skills practised through classifying shapes can help children to classify numbers according to their properties. Teachers have to make this connection for children.

2D shapes

We can classify 2D shapes according to whether their *sides* are **straight** or **curved**. Those with **curved** sides are generally familiar to children – a *circle* (e.g. the face of a clock) and a *semicircle* are the main plane shapes with curved sides that children will consider at primary level. An *oval* or *ellipse* is a familiar shape to children from their writing of the letter 'o' and the symbol for zero, but its mathematical properties are not considered at this stage.

A 2D **straight**-sided closed shape is called a *polygon*. Polygons can be classified according to:

- the number of sides of the polygon – *triangles* three sides, *quadrilaterals* four sides, *pentagons* five sides etc.;
- regularity – polygons can be regular or irregular. They are regular when all the sides are the same length and all the angles the same size.

Further classification is possible of triangles and quadrilaterals. Triangles can be classified according to their sides – *equilateral* (all sides equal length), *isosceles* (two sides equal length), *scalene* (no equal sides). Also, we consider their angles – *acute* (less than 90 degrees), *obtuse* (more than 90 degrees), *right-angled* (90 degrees), *reflex* (more than 180 degrees).

Similarly, quadrilaterals can be classified into those that have parallel sides and those that do not. The majority of the quadrilaterals we use have at least one pair of parallel sides. A further refinement of definition could separate out those quadrilaterals into those with no parallel sides, those with one pair of parallel sides and those with two pairs of parallel sides, known as parallelograms. These parallelograms can then be further subdivided through the additional definition of whether or not they have internal right angles and/or whether or not any of their sides are of equal length.

Hence, a square is a parallelogram.

Can you first list all parallelograms and second, classify them according to their characteristics? (While a square is a subset of rectangles, an oblong is used to describe a rectangle that is not a square.)

There are a few quadrilaterals which are not parallelograms. A *trapezium* has one pair of sides that are parallel and a *kite* has two pairs of sides of equal length and one line of symmetry.

2D shapes can be classified according to whether they *tessellate* (the same shape fitting together with others without leaving any spaces) or whether they have lines of *reflective symmetry* (whether they could be folded on a line so that one half fits exactly on top of the other half) or *rotational symmetry* (see 'Understanding properties of position and movement' on page 72).

You can probably see that many familiar shapes fit into a range of classifications. Take, for example, a square. It is a regular polygon, has four sides of equal length, opposite sides are parallel and it has four right-angles. If we wanted an *exclusive* definition of a square we would have to include the majority of these classifications. However, if we were to take out the requirement of right-angles and being a regular polygon then we could have a more *inclusive* definition allowing rhombi to be incorporated. The more properties defined the more *exclusive* the definition.

3D shapes

3D shapes can be similarly defined as 2D shapes but will also include the 2D shapes of the faces. We can classify 3D shapes according to whether their surfaces are **flat** or **curved**. Those with **curved** surfaces are generally familiar to children – a *sphere* being a ball shape and half a sphere a *hemisphere*, a *cylinder* as in a baked-bean tin, and a *cone* that we use with ice-cream.

A 3D **flat** surface is called a *face*, the lines where the two faces meet are called *edges* and the points where the edges meet are called *vertices* (singular *vertex*). The shape is called a *polyhedron*. Polyhedra can then be classified according to:

- the number of faces of the polygon;
- regularity – polyhedra can be regular or irregular. They are regular when all the faces are the same regular 2D shape, all the edges are the same length and all the angles between the edges are equal. There are only five regular polyhedra and these are called the platonic solids. A cube fulfils the criteria for a platonic solid. Each face of the cube is a square. The other four platonic solids (tetrahedron, octahedron, dodecahedron and icosahedron) have either equilateral triangles or regular pentagons as their faces.

> Using plastic construction materials, make the other four platonic solids. Consider the year groups you could use this activity with. How could you connect it to other curriculum subjects?

Other 3 D shapes can be classified according to:

- Whether they are made from two identical polygons at either end. These shapes are called *prisms*.
- Whether they have a polygon at the base and lines from each of the vertices from this polygon that meet at point called an *apex*. These shapes are called *pyramids*.

3D shapes can be further classified by *planes of symmetry* – a plane that divides the shape into halves that are mirror images of each other. Curved shapes have an infinite number of planes of symmetry whereas flat-faced shapes have a defined number.

> Make a cube from plasticine. Find out how many single cuts you can make so that each part is a mirror image of each other. Now compare this with a sphere.

Interestingly, the 3D equivalent of tessellation – shapes that fit together without leaving spaces such as cubes and cuboids – are not referred to generally apart from when considering packaging. However, examples are around us all the time such as bricks in the wall.

Nets and geometric constructions

One connection between 2D and 3D shapes is when 3D shapes are constructed, as shown earlier with respect to platonic solids. This can be extended to drawing a 2D *net* of 3D shapes when the understanding and perceptions of the children can be developed through deconstruction as well as construction of the physical materials, allowing them to develop 2D plans or nets. Other geometric constructions at primary level involve using increasing awareness of properties to construct shapes on paper and with construction materials.

> Look at the connections given in the geography National Curriculum links, Key Stages 1 and 2 to the shape and space parts of the mathematics National Curriculum.

Your teaching

We live in a three-dimensional world and shape is all around us. The emphasis in the National Curriculum is on introducing two-dimensional work before three-dimensional work. However, we initially learn about the properties of 3D shapes by what they can do such as rolling and stacking. At the Foundation Stage children need a range of informal experiences such as play with construction toys and making models that give them the opportunity to describe the shape and size of 2D and 3D shapes.

Work at primary level can be broadly classified in three areas: (1) describing and sorting 2D and 3D shapes, (2) making shapes and patterns and (3) symmetry. As has been stated earlier, although this is a topic with a strong visual element, connections need to be made to language and number in the form of defining properties. A useful connection can be made to number work – by giving children experiences of shape they can form mental images. This should complement their visualisation of number lines and squares and vice versa.

Notation/language	Representation
Describing and sorting 2D and 3D shapes.	3D objects such as cars, plastic farmyard animals etc; 3D shapes that roll, slide or stack.
Classification – activities for sorting with growing awareness of identifying properties and the relationship between them.	Plastic shapes, geoboards, pipe cleaners, straws – work with a variety of shapes including irregular shapes, both convex and concave, presented in different orientations so that children can develop their understanding of properties and can use the related vocabulary. Relating 2D and 3D shapes to their everyday equivalents extends learning opportunities. Making pictures with gummed shapes and flannel graphs and objects with construction toys encourages children to consider the properties of shape and in a group situation develops discussion. Everyday examples of shapes such as food and domestic packaging are useful for exploring the surfaces and are easy for children to handle. Opening out a tissue box is a helpful introduction to a net at a later stage. Activities that give opportunities to relate 3D models to 2D representation such as following a Lego diagram help children with visualisation. This should support children in visualising number lines, squares and patterns as well as being able to visualise the nets of shapes.
Progression in classification is important if children are to identify a range of properties. Relating right-angles to a quarter turn. The sum of angles at a point and on a straight line.	Apart from construction of shapes such work can be consolidated by PE (moving through a quarter, half and full turn) and geography (points of the compass) as it particularly emphasises the dynamic rather than static aspect of angles. Another excellent tool for developing children's understanding of the dynamics and extent of turning is the Roamer©.
Reasoning and investigations. Work with shape is helpful for developing skills of reasoning as it has an intrinsic kinaesthetic aspect that may support children in their understanding of reasoning with number.	Use of pictures and diagrams of 3D shapes in ways that encourage children to visualise and reason about them.

Symmetry: identifying and making symmetrical images.

Using a range of ICT programmes to form symmetrical shapes and using the facility to rotate shapes. Links to other aspects of the curriculum such as art and PE.

The children's learning

Assessment opportunities need to include examples of shapes that are not regular or in familiar orientations. As children develop their understanding of shape they need to relate the properties of shape to a visual image. For example, rather than just rely on recognising a square they need to apply their knowledge that a square has four right-angles and four sides of the same length so the following shapes can be both identified as squares (Fig. 3.2).

Figure 3.2

Shape work also allows for opportunities to assess children's ability to visualise whether it is a shape, a number or number within a shape as in a number line or 100 square.

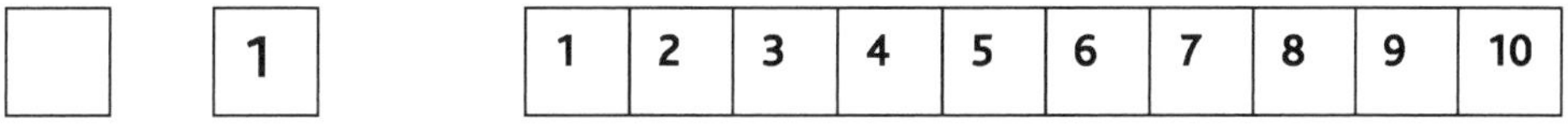

Figure 3.3

Understanding of concepts such as conservation and classification can also be assessed by work with properties of shape.

Summary

- There is a distinct terminology concerned with the properties of shape that children need to apply accurately.
- Children progress from identifying shapes by their physical appearance to identification through properties that can be classified.
- Children need to be presented with shapes that are both regular and irregular in a range of orientations.
- Work with shape enables children to relate conservation, classification and equivalence to other areas of mathematics and so consolidate their understanding.

Understanding properties of position and movement

Introduction

When we teach shape, we tend to teach two dimensions (2D) first and then three dimensions (3D), probably because 2 is a lower number than 3. However, in child development terms, 2D is much more abstract than 3D. A developing child relates to the world around him by where he is in relation to everything else. He puts objects into his mouth to try to understand them. He will reach out and touch to find out information and he will then move to attain what he wants. All this illustrates that we live in a 3D world and therefore this is relevant to us in a way that 2D never will be. The use of 2D in the context of position and movement is mainly that of representation.

When a child wants to work out where he is, he uses his senses to find markers that give clues as to where he is in relation to them. One marker is helpful but two or more determines his location with increasing accuracy. As adults, we still use these markers and, depending on how familiar our surroundings are, we use various strategies and support mechanisms to aid our mental mapping of our position. This is the basis from which to plan teaching of position and movement. There are a great many possibilities for connections and equivalence – this section will explore just some of those links and possibilities.

Your mathematics

Location

The adage that women cannot read maps seems to have a grain of truth, if reporting in the media is to be believed. Ongoing research into the functions of the different part of the brain – and in particular the right and left hemispheres – suggests that in general, the brains of men and women do function differently. Of course, there are many women who are good map-readers and many men who are not so we must not fall into the trap of using stereotypes to establish self-fulfilling prophesies.

> How would you assess your map-reading ability? What are your indicators for your assessment? (How do you know?)

It is worth breaking down the features of map-reading to see what it is that we can or cannot do (always keeping in mind the nature–nurture argument).

> First, from where you are sitting, with your eyes open choose an object (such as a book). Describe where it is located.
>
> What do you say? Is it structured or random information? Is it meaningful to you but perhaps less so to someone else?

Repeat the exercise with a friend. Both pick the same object and separately note down information that is relevant to its location. How much have you each noted that is similar and how much is different? Did you or your friend note anything that the other had not even noticed?

Now try closing your eyes. In a different place from the above: how much of your present surroundings can you locate? Open your eyes. How accurate were you?

Now imagine you are in familiar surroundings and are asked to give directions to a particular landmark. What will you say? What pictures do you have in your mind while you are saying it? How much do you use your body as part of your communication? How accurate do you think you are?

With all of the above, regardless of how good you were at it, you were using a myriad of subconscious skills and knowledge, learned both through experience and through being taught. In addition to being able to describe the position of your chosen target, you were also probably using directional information to enhance your description and to guide yourself or your enquirer to the target. The vocabulary used may not have been sophisticated navigational language, but it was probably sufficient for the purpose.

The difficulties that arise (if they do) with map-reading can be laid at the door of the change from the reality of 3D to the abstraction of 2D. A map is a representation of the reality, which requires the reader to interpret a range of different symbols and relate them to what they would expect to find if they visited that place. The notation chosen for these symbols will vary according to its purpose, but a key ensures that you have possession of all relevant information.

Return to the notes you made when describing the location of a particular object. What representation did you use? Did you choose any particular form of notation? Do you feel comfortable working with a plan or do you prefer to hear the information and to form your own mental picture?

If you are a visual sort of person, you may have already chosen to represent your notes in graphic form, i.e. a plan or crude map. But if you have not already done so, do it now. How useful do you think your plan is? Does it locate your chosen object from any position in the room? How do you know how to orientate your plan? When you read a map, do you feel the need to turn it so it is facing the way you are in reality?

The next stage of communication of position and movement is to use a standardised notation such that another person with the same map can have unequivocal information, enabling them to locate exactly what you mean. The common form of noting position on a plan or map is through co-ordinates in the form of grid references with two parts and for movement, range and bearing. Range is, of course, a measure and this is discussed later in this chapter. Both grid references and range and bearing give 2D information.

> How is the map-user given information about the 3D reality? What representation and notation is used?
>
> Consider the stages briefly examined above, from seeing where something is, through remembering in your mind's eye to following a map or plan in an unknown situation. Is there a stage at which your confidence in your skills, knowledge or understanding breaks down?

The kinaesthetic understanding of position and movement that comes as normal development in childhood translates easily, for some, into the skill of using 2D explanations through representations and notations. But for others, it does not come so naturally.

> If your understanding (shown through difficulty in applying) of the representation and notation of position and movement would benefit from development, think of ways in which you can use what you can understand to develop that which you cannot.

The consideration of the role and purpose of maps is only one way to evaluate our facility with understanding position and movement.

> From your own experiences, can you think of other examples or situations?

Transformations

Another perspective of movement is that of transformation. In primary mathematics terms, this can be considered as the movement of a 2D shape. This movement is described in one of four ways:

- reflection;
- rotation;
- translation;
- enlargement.

While these transformations can be described numerically through co-ordinates, the focus of the work at the primary level is the visual effect achieved. Enlargement speaks for itself – the shape becomes larger (or smaller if a negative factor is applied), retaining angle size and proportion of side lengths. The two shapes are similar.

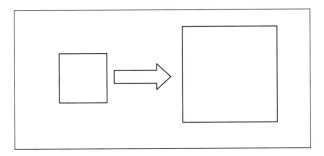

Figure 3.4

Reflection, rotation and translation do not involve changing the size of the shape, although a reflected shape cannot be considered congruent whereas a rotated or translated shape can. The deconstruction of a transformation offers interesting possibilities depending on the shape and which of these three transformations or combination of transformations is chosen.

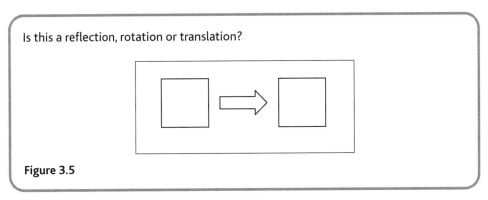

Is this a reflection, rotation or translation?

Figure 3.5

If we have more information, it becomes easier to analyse.

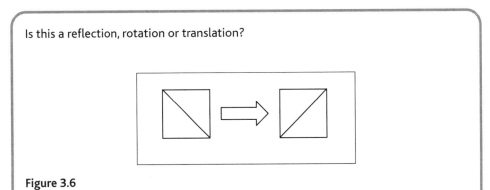

Is this a reflection, rotation or translation?

Figure 3.6

If it is a reflection, where is the line of symmetry? If it is a rotation, where might be the centre of rotation? Through how many degrees is it rotated? Could it be a translation followed by a rotation or reflection? Can you see how these might be possibilities?

Reflection can often be determined visually but rotation is harder to visualise, especially if the centre of rotation is outside the shape as it would be with the above example.

Familiar uses of transformation include tiling and wallpaper design. The artist creates the basic design which is then transformed repeatedly. While this has traditionally been done manually, nowadays it is usually achieved using computer-generated design. Tiling designs have been used throughout history and can be found in locations all over the world.

> Do you have any tiling in the buildings with which you are familiar? Seemingly complex designs usually have a foundation in a basic 2D shape such as a square or rhombus.
>
> When choosing a tiling pattern, what is the starting shape? Is there more than one? How is it (or are they) moved and repeated to create the tiling pattern? How did you work this out?

We can start to deconstruct a wallpaper design to decide the basic design and the transformations undertaken. One way to do this is to look at the pattern repeat information on the wrapper.

> Choose a wallpaper with a simple pattern with a small pattern repeat. Can you find the basic pattern? Can you draw the basic shape within which it is drawn? When you trace the basic pattern, can you find where it repeats and what transformation it has undergone?

Your teaching

As teachers, we draw on a range of resources to support effective teaching and hence effective learning, of which the most important resource is ourselves. Your knowledge and understanding of position and movement enables you to plan to teach using the children's natural strengths while acknowledging where errors and misconceptions may creep in.

> Using the statutory (National Curriculum) and advisory (NNS) documents, list the expected progression for position and movement.
>
> At what stage are you asked to move the children into representation and notation? From your experience, where are the main points when errors or misconceptions may occur?

The point from which your teaching needs to start is from the child's understanding of his/her own body and position and movement relative to that. As discussed above, this kinaesthetic understanding remains the basis of confidence through into adulthood, therefore regardless of the level of attainment and ages of the children, it should be an integral part of your planning and teaching.

For each objective identified in the progression above, determine how it can be related kinaesthetically to the expected learning, drawing on theories of how children learn.

Objective	Kinaesthetic connections

Figure 3.7

In what ways are these connections related to cross-mathematical and cross-curricular links? How can you build these links into your overall planning to give continuity to the children's experiences, taking into consideration such aspects as zone of proximal development (ZPD) (Vygotsky 1978), scaffolding and a spirally based curriculum?

One of the teaching tools available is cognitive conflict. This works on the principle of offering the children something that challenges their existing understanding, so encouraging them to reason. Challenging children's understanding of how they determine position and movement in relation to their bodies allows them to consider objectively that which they have always accepted without conscious thought.

Look again at your response to kinaesthetic connections. How could these be developed to include some cognitive conflict, enabling mental interrogation of physical responses?

Besides yourself as a resource, there are many resources available to support your teaching of position and movement. For example, cross-curricular links have already been considered.

What resources have you come across that encourage teaching kinaesthetically?

ICT

Have you included ICT? Consider the program Logo. The various hardware and software available supports progression throughout the primary age range from the use of a floor turtle to replicate the direct connections of body to position and movement to on-screen, interactive computer programs that can be used to develop skills in all aspects of position and movement.

Describe the ICT you have already come across, which of the objectives it met and how it supported teaching.

Objective	ICT	How does it support teaching?

Figure 3.8

Now consider resources such as mathematics schemes (both commercially and school produced) including textbooks and photocopiable worksheets.

Look through a scheme that you have worked with or might like to. How closely does it follow the progression you determined upon earlier in this section? How many of the suggested activities and exercises, given to meet objectives, are kinaesthetically based? How well does the scheme help you to teach the transition from concrete through visual to abstract? How useful is it as a teaching resource to help with medium-term and weekly planning? Will you have to make many adaptations or changes?

The grouping arrangements for this work will need a bit of thought. Ability in position and movement is not necessarily the same as in general numeracy. Therefore it is worth making assessments at each teaching stage to determine what stage of understanding each child has reached. Rate of development will not just be a result of their natural abilities and their assimilation of previously taught work – out-of-school activities such as Cubs and Brownies and membership of sports clubs will also have an effect and it is worth including information on these in your assessment.

For your class, list the children's outside interests. How might they contribute to the child's understanding of position and movement?

Next, the standardised representation and notation of position and movement needs to be considered. As previously mentioned, this is achieved through co-ordinates and bearing and range.

Co-ordinates

Co-ordinates allow a position to be pinpointed to whatever degree of accuracy is appropriate. From the developmental point of view, this moves the child on from the potentially ambiguous: 'It's next to the teacher's desk, to the right as you look at it and just before the noticeboard starts.' There is nothing wrong with this system which is usually sufficient for our needs on a day-to-day basis. But a co-ordinate system removes the ambiguity and sets in place the common language of mathematics.

While the abilities of the children in position and movement may differ from the numerical abilities, co-ordinates through grid references will reinforce and support over-learning of place value in a different context. Simple grid references can start with alpha-numeric grids in which the spaces are labelled. This enables the child to locate his target to within the area of the referenced square. Grid referencing can then be developed right up to the point of longitude and latitude on a global scale.

> List the progression in grid referencing that takes the children from simple to complex. Does your list show linear progression from everyday, familiar and directly related to themselves for the simpler representation to realms beyond their own experience? Can you determine how the familiar, contextualised element can be used to teach at each level?

Turning

Turns are movements that change direction. As with location, adults as well as children often use everyday language and gestures to explain what they mean, especially when talking with someone. For example, a child may say: 'Go along there until you get to the corner and then turn that way' while indicating with his arm the direction of the turn. This will work either in the actual location or when planning a route using a map. In development of the mathematical understanding of moving from the present course to be able to find the target, more specific vocabulary needs to be introduced. A start can be made with left and right, which sometimes need more teaching time and consideration than anticipated, regardless of a child's mathematical ability. Turning to the left and right is a good example of how it is necessary to learn kinaesthetically so the child can feel what it means and so can understand. The need to decide the direction of turn is the point at which so many children often encounter difficulty. The child is not only being asked to work from a plan, so translating the kinaesthetic into visualisation, but also to accommodate a map orientation that may be different to his own.

> How many ways can you think of to help a child to develop the necessary mental orientation that will enable him to be able confidently to determine right and left turns, regardless of the alignment of the plan or map?

The usual progression is then to continue through compass points with increasing accuracy, such as north and south, north-west and south-west to bearings that give the required heading to a target such as 060°. This is less confusing, however, in map-reading terms for a child than the apparently simple turn to left and right. Bearings and headings are located on a fixed orientation, i.e. north, and therefore can be related much more easily to a diagrammatic representation of the reality, i.e. the map.

> In the mathematics scheme you looked at earlier, how does it tackle progression in measuring direction?

Of course not all turns are undertaken on the spot as suggested, with only the body rotating. Many are part of a directional movement and by the completion of the turn you may have moved some distance. This further aspect of moving from one position to another creates some interesting connections with other areas of mathematics such as shape. And it becomes even more interesting if the target is moving. In this way, you can extend your teaching on position and movement while creating the possibilities of challenging dynamic visual imagery.

Imagine, using Figure 3.9, that a mouse is running along the bottom side of a 10-metre square garden. A cat chases it at the same speed.

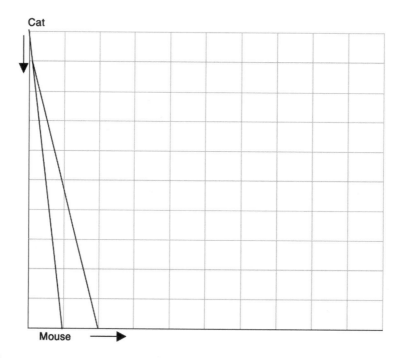

Figure 3.9

Plot, as indicated, the position of the mouse and the cat for each metre they travel. What is the resultant course of the cat? How can this be taught kinaesthetically using the children themselves to help their understanding? What resources might be useful to develop this concept visually?

Type 'curved pursuit' into an Internet search engine. What do you find?

Transformations

Teaching transformations develops the children's visualisation skills. Use of resources can help with the process, such as a mirror for reflection and tracing paper for rotation. When choosing illustrative examples for the children to analyse, whether prepared by you or drawn from commercial materials such as wallpapers, you need to take care that the lines of symmetry and centres of rotation are simple. In particular, for rotation it is best to have the centre of rotation as either the centre of the shape/design or on one of the corners – anything else is too complex (although could be used as extension work for the more able children).

If you looked at wallpapers earlier in this chapter, did you find one with an 'easy' centre of rotation?

Children can help their mastery of the concepts and related vocabulary through a range of construction and deconstruction work such as:

- Using simple shapes such as rectangles and triangles, perhaps modified by a line or spot, to explore the effects of each transformation and a combination of transformations.
- Creating a single transformation of a shape and then passing it to a partner for deconstruction.
- Creating a single transformation of a shape and then describing it, using appropriate vocabulary, for a partner to draw without seeing it.
- Creating a tiling pattern from one shape with one transformation and then developing this to include different transformations, different basic shapes, more than one transformation and more than one shape.
- Creating a wallpaper design both manually and using a graphics program.

Can you think of any others?

The children's learning

Throughout this chapter, the focus has been on how, through your teaching, you can help children to use the normal development of their physical senses of position and movement to learn to understand them from a mathematical perspective.

A child's acceptance of his body's ability to locate himself in relation to his surroundings is the starting point for his learning. Understanding of this ability can be taught through a range of strategies, some of which come through other curriculum areas and may be unconscious learning. In order to evaluate the effectiveness of this learning, assessment needs to be devised that will enable the child to make explicit his understanding.

> Consider the different ways in which the children could communicate their understanding to you. Would you accept kinaesthetic communication? How would you record it?
>
> How could you use cross-curricular work to give relevance to the children's learning?

> Return to your original table of objectives, bearing in mind the three levels of curriculum: the planned, the taught and the learned. Would you make any changes to the table? How would you assess the learning of each stage? How would you plan to develop or provide extra support as determined through assessment?

Summary

- Position and movement are a fairly small part of the mathematics curriculum. However, it is easily related directly to the out-of-school world of the child and therefore is available to be used as a vehicle for teaching and learning a wide range of connected mathematical concepts.

- Through effective teaching, the child can learn how to connect his instinctive use of his body to locate position and to undertake movement with visual representation, mental imagery and abstract notations.

Understanding measures

Introduction

'How far is it from the school to the bus stop?' – 'About 5 minutes'. 'How much petrol did you put in the car?' – '£10'. We use measures in a multitude of ways: conventional and unconventional, standard and non-standard, metric and imperial. The nature of the measures we choose depends on a number of factors including our own understanding, that of the audience and the situation in which we are required to use measures. In space travel, distance is measured in the time it takes light to travel, which reduces immense distances to something we can at least represent in manageable numbers. Measures pervade the daily lives of children although most of the time they are unaware of them, using measures unthinkingly.

This chapter will examine our understanding of measures including representation and notation, the role of estimation and approximation and the connections that can be made both within the mathematics curriculum and across other subjects.

Your mathematics

Consider the last few days. List the last ten occasions when you used measures. Did any of these occasions cause you to use estimation and how accurate do you think you were? Were you accurate enough for your purposes or did you then need to check? If you did check, how did you decide what instrument was best suited to the task? How did you know how to use the instrument? Did you use non-standard, imperial or metric scales?

The questions above are all intended to get you to look at yourself as a user of measures. We measure many things, for example:

- Length (which includes such things as height and distance) and then area and volume.
- Capacity (which differs from volume).
- Mass (which is not the same as weight).
- Angles (which is an amount of turn).
- Time (about which Einstein had a theory or two).
- Temperature (when o does not mean nothing).
- Value (which concerns money but offers opportunities for deeper philosophical discussion).
- Compound measures such as rate.

What is the difference between capacity and volume? What is the difference between mass and weight? Why do we use weight incorrectly in everyday language? How important do you think this is?

The way in which we express measures is often also how we define them. For example, time is so deeply abstract that we can only define it practically through the units of measure and the mechanics of the measuring instrument, both human constructs, to endeavour to quantify the unquantifiable.

Consider this list above and any others you have thought of. Are you able to define each as an entity? Which do you find yourself defining through the units of measure or the instrument?

Our familiarity with measures in everyday use enables us to make choices to suit both us and the situation. This often includes mixing non-standard, imperial and metric scales which, in general, most people understand. Consider preparing to go on holiday. The brochure tells us about a variety of measured information which may include:

- Costs, including offers and discounts, in £s.
- Flight times in hours and minutes.
- Luggage weight limits in kilos for hold luggage and dimensions for hand luggage in centimetres.
- Distance of the resort from the airport in miles or hours/minutes.
- Resort temperature, either in °F or °C (or both).
- Local currency.
- Size of the swimming pool in either feet or metres.

The scales of measure indicated here are a mix of non-standard, imperial and metric. In addition, the measured information may be represented in different ways such as graphs, charts, maps, comparative tables and narrative (which may contain words and numeric values).

For many of us brought up with imperial measures, the metric scales still have little meaning. We often estimate much more securely in old, familiar scales and, in general, only become comfortable and familiar with metric measures if we have cause to use them regularly and frequently.

Consider the list of things we measured considered earlier, using the chart started below (Fig. 3.10). How much can you fill in from your own knowledge with a sense of confidence? Can you fill it all in with help? For each, which measuring system (metric or imperial) do you feel most confident using?

Within both metric and imperial measures, the units of measure are related through bases. The metric system has been designed to work solely on base 10, for example, there are 10mm in 1 cm. This, of course, relates directly to the use of place value in our counting system. However, the imperial system works on many bases, which evolved through history.

From your list in Figure 3.10, can you determine which bases are used for each imperial system? (For example, there are 12 inches in a foot, therefore feet are in base 12.) If it interests you, find out some of the history behind the old systems.

Measure	Metric	Imperial	Approx. equivalences
Length	mm cm m km	inch foot yard mile	2½cm ≈ 1 inch 30cm ≈ 1 foot 1m ≈ 1 yard 1km ≈ 5/8 mile
Area			
Volume			
Capacity			
Mass			
Angles			
Time			
Value			
Temperature			
Speed			

Figure 3.10

Your teaching

Children initially measure using non-standard units that are available (i.e. themselves) to answer such questions as how many footsteps across the room or how many marbles can they hold in their hands. Therefore this should be the starting point for formalising their understanding. There are four basic principles of measure which, while not strictly hierarchical, can be considered to follow on one from the other in terms of the child's developing understanding:

1   Comparing magnitude in which the vocabulary moves from such as small and big to bigger and biggest.

2   Transitivity, which can be summarised as: if A is bigger than B and B is bigger than C, then C is bigger than A.

3   Conservation, which considers retention or change of characteristics if, for example, position or shape change.

4   How many of a given number to make a total, as in how many steps around the playground or how many centimetres to the edge.

There is also the need to consider the possibilities for errors and misconceptions that may arise at any stage of the child's developing understanding. For example, when using pinboards for shape work, the distance between two pins on the side of the square is generally considered one unit (standard units are not appropriate here). In many cases, however, the child's natural extension of this is also to call the diagonal distance between two pins one unit.

Using the earlier list, how many examples of errors or misconceptions can you think of from your own teaching experience? Which generally arise as errors and which as misconceptions? How might you teach to avoid them occurring? Are there any that you might use for the teaching strategy of cognitive conflict?

Development of skills should form a significant part of your teaching in measures. These, in general, comprise:

- the practical skills of the correct and accurate use of the instruments of measure;
- the skills to make decisions about which measures, and hence instruments, to use;
- the skill of estimation.

All of the three skills areas are of importance with none coming first and none being independent of the other two.

Instrument use

The skills associated with the use of instruments need to be taught and practised throughout the primary school to help ensure confidence and competence. Consider, once again, the list of measures at the start of this section. For each, note down the instruments of measure (non-standard and standard) that might be used. Use this as an opportunity to look for connections through choice of instrument.

At what stage of the child's development would you teach the use of each? How would you introduce the standard measuring instruments as a development from non-standard instruments? In each case, what would you have to emphasise to avoid unnecessary inaccuracies?

Choices

The skills of choice are related to the use of instruments. All measures are approximations and we need to teach the children to make reasoned decisions about the level of accuracy that is appropriate in each situation. This means that teaching of skills for the use of instruments of measures should be complemented by teaching how to make the best choice of unit of measure and instrument. Also part of the skill of choice is to choose how accurate is 'reasonable'. This has implications for the teaching of scale and this, in turn, is related to place value. Of course, the intervals on the scales used will be related to the base unit of measure.

When planning a lesson, how do you plan to develop the children's skills in deciding how accurately to measure? How often do you make those decisions for the children, how often do you support their decision-making and how often do you leave the choice entirely up to them for learning through trial and improvement?

Choose a lesson in which one of your objectives is to develop skills in making choices. What probing questions could you ask to support the skill development? What role would discussion have in supporting the children's decisions? How would you use formative assessment to determine differentiation needs?

Estimation

The third skill noted is that of estimation. From earliest childhood we estimate and refine this skill practically as a natural part of our development. For example, a non-walking child will learn whether a toy is within reach from experience gained through trial and improvement and it is this instinct that should be exploited in teaching. In particular, the 'improvement' should provide the teacher with an opportunity for conscious skills development. There is little value in a child estimating the length of six classroom objects and then measuring them to check for accuracy. There is much more value in the estimation of the length of the first object, measuring it (with due consideration of the reasonable accuracy required), comparing the measure with the estimate, consciously determining the nature of the error and using that to estimate the length of the next object. In addition, encouraging choice in the order of estimation enables the child to develop estimation skills both through comparing magnitude and through transitivity.

How do you help the children you teach to develop their skills of estimation?

Mental images help with estimation and it is important that we use the familiar, non-standard images to help move children towards confidence and competence in standard units. For example, on a visit to a historic ship, children will be most unlikely to be able to relate to the fact that the ship is 420 feet (or even 120 metres) long. Therefore, in that form it will have little meaning to them. But if that fact is used in conjunction with a context that uses real-life equivalence, the children will be able to add it to their own mental images. Thus the length can be related to about 10 buses end-to-end or the same as a football pitch.

Considering the list again, do you know what mental images the children might have that could be used to help them to relate unfamiliar measures to their world? How can you use reference material, including the Internet, to help children to improve their estimation skills?

An application of simple measures is to compound measures. For example, a measure of distance compared with a measure of time allows us to determine speed, and a measure of mass compared with a measure of volume gives a measure of density. The notation of compound measure reflects both (or all, if more than two are involved) of the contributory measures, which leads to potential disorientation if different units of measure are used. For example, 56 miles per hour (mph) is the same as 25 metres per second, but given both, we would not be able to relate one to the other without conversions involving calculations of several stages or the use of conversion charts. However, the notation can also support the decision for calculation choice as mph can also be written m/h. This, of course, indicates division – another useful connection.

> What other compound measures are relevant to your teaching? What teaching opportunities have you come across to develop the necessary understanding? What examples can you think of that would make it possible to teach conversions of compound measures in a context relevant to the children?

Notation and representation

The notation and representation of measures reinforces learning of not only the knowledge, skills and understanding of measures, but also of other areas of mathematics. In particular, place value benefits from repeated over-learning through the use of the metric measure system. Multiplication and division by multiples of ten within each system of measure will contextualise the whole number and decimal aspects of our base 10 counting system.

For example, a length of 0.6m would be expressed as 600mm for many household uses and crafts such as carpentry and yet for children, 60cm may be easier to visualise as the width of their table. But as they all mean the same length, the choice of notation is individual and context relevant.

Similarly, when money is put into the context of place value, then it becomes much easier for the children to grasp that an amount can be written as a number of pounds, including fractional parts (e.g. £3.62) or as a number of pence (362p). The error in notation that often arises of putting signs for both pounds and pence in the same number can be explained once the decimal fraction is understood. Of course, it is reasonable to say, 'Three pounds and sixty-two pence' as each part is considered as separate units. Children can learn that this verbal habit is the legacy from the days of imperial measures when the bases varied within units of measure and each unit therefore was written down, e.g. £5 7s 8d, although this was often shortened to £5/7/8 or a version thereof (where the / does not mean division).

> How could you use calculations in these different bases as a means of assessing the children's understanding of place value? What, if any, errors and misconceptions in notation have you noticed with the children you teach? How can you use these to develop their understanding of place value?

The children's learning

The main discussion of teaching in measures has been through the development of confidence and competence in skills, with little mention made of knowledge or understanding. For some measures, the knowledge can be gained from the skills as children practise and use them. Much of the discussion that is generated from lessons to improve abilities in choice and use of instrument, accuracy and estimation will include opportunities for teaching knowledge and understanding.

> Refer back to some of the skills planning discussed in the teaching part of this section. How could you plan specifically and explicitly for learning in knowledge and understanding?

Some parts of measures are more abstract than others and consequently take some children much longer to reach a level of understanding. Time is one such measure. In this situation, the learned skill in the use of the instrument at least allows the child to know what the instrument is telling him so that through practice, he can develop an understanding of the relevance of that to his everyday life. The comparison of what the clock is telling him with events in the day, such as lunch, will mean that he will have learned to tell the time at a functional and useful level. He can also use this skill to compare with others who also have a clock and therefore arrive at the same place at the same time.

Children's learning can often be evidenced through their application of what they know, understand and can do in different situations. In measures, one such example of this could be through the challenge of measuring inaccessible heights. The skills of simple measures we teach are generally concerned with the physical act of applying the instrument of measure directly to the thing being measured. However, if this cannot be done then other means must be used.

> What knowledge, skills and understandings would a child be able to demonstrate when determining the height of the church tower? What other situations can you think of that allow children to demonstrate their application and transference of their learning?

Summary

- The functional understanding of measures generally arises out of confidence and competence in the knowledge of the different systems for measure and the relevant and appropriate instruments of measure, and of skills in their use and application.

- Understanding of measures in a more abstract sense develops throughout childhood at different rates for each child according to need and relevance.

Thus, our natural non-standard measure systems are always of relevance as the context within which development of understanding takes place. Equally, familiarity with both imperial and metric systems and their approximate equivalence adds a flexibility to the children's opportunities that encompass learning both within and outside school.

- Estimation forms an important, central role in effective learning about measures as from this the children can learn to make decisions about such things as degree of accuracy, appropriateness of unit of measure, choice of instrument and selection of known information to determine the unknown.

CHAPTER 4

Handling data

SOME KEY CONNECTIONS WITHIN AND ACROSS ATTAINMENT TARGETS

- Forms of graphical representation.
- Types of average.
- Problem-solving in the planning stage of handling data.
- Probability and fractional notation.
- Scales, measurement and handling data.

Using and applying handling data

Introduction

Data, in its many forms including probability, impacts daily on our lives. We see data in the news, in the papers, on cereal packets, in science reports . . . the list goes on. The way in which this data is handled, either by us or by someone else, greatly influences our understanding of what is being presented. The use of data-handling computer programs has also made effective presentation and interpretation much more accessible to primary school-aged children. Therefore it is in their interests, in line with the old adage 'a little bit of knowledge is a dangerous thing' that we teach our children the knowledge, skills and understanding to deal with and use data appropriately.

There are five stages of handling data (although you will come across variations):

1 Ask the question – what do you want to find out?

2 Make a plan – what data will help to answer the question?

3 Collect the data.

4 Present the data – what form is best suited to the type of data and to enable you to answer the question?

5 Interpret the data to answer the question.

Experiences of handling data in out-of-school settings may well be considered as part of stage 5. Much of the data we meet in everyday lives is concerned with information that has already been collected and presented. Often, an interpretation is offered based on what the writer wants you to know.

Other experiences of handling data that is more specific to teachers include deciding which type of graph is best suited to the age of the children with all the attendant elements such as scale or how best to present findings in science lessons. For many, the aforementioned computer programs may appear to make these decisions easier, but as with all technology, uncertainty in subject knowledge can place an over-reliance on the computer to make decisions, which may not be the best or appropriate.

Your mathematics

> Can you list any data you have come across, outside the classroom, in the last week?
>
> With which of the five stages noted above did you need to be actively engaged? For each of the stages, can you think of examples of representation and notation you have come across, outside the classroom?

When considering data such as that in Figure 4.1, there many pathways that can be taken to answer many questions. More often than not, it is necessary to be selective, choosing what is important for you to know so you can determine what you will do as a result of this analysis.

> What have you come across recently that has presented you with selected data and interpretation? What else would you have liked to have known to get a fuller picture?
>
> Why have the authors chosen to present their findings to their audience in this way?

Most routine requirements for data that we come across tend to be the interpretation of the information presented. Even then the accompanying narrative offers an interpretation, with the presented data being used to justify the conclusions drawn.

> When you are presented with data, do you find it easier to interpret if it is in tabular, graphical or narrative form?

Stage	Representation	Notation
1 Ask the question	e.g. How do my school's SATs results compare with last year's? How do they relate to the start of year targets?	e.g.
2 Make a plan	e.g. ● Do I want to know KS1 and KS 2? ● Do I want to track individual children/years?	e.g.
3 Collect the data	e.g. ● Panda report. ● Own data – levels achieved this year and last + target levels set.	e.g.
4 Present the data	e.g. Using Excel, record data for: ● last year's KS1 SATs ● this year's KS1 SATs ● this year's KS1 targets ● this year's KS1 TAs on one bar chart (discrete data).	e.g.
5 Interpret the data	e.g. ● Is there improvement in SATs results throughout? ● Is it at the top end – bottom end? ● How good are our targets? ● How close are our TAs to the SATs and the targets? ● Were our targets over/under ambitious or was it the SATs? ● What are the implications for next year?	e.g.

Figure 4.1

When you have raw data to work with, how comfortable are you with:

● Determining the most appropriate chart or graph and drawing it?

● Calculating averages and deciding whether mean, mode or median suits your purpose best?

● Deciding whether percentages are useful and how then to calculate fractions and percentages?

● Determining probability for various outcomes?

Your teaching

Although the five stages of handling data are noted as separate, it can be seen that they all form part of a continuum with the different elements being of greater or less importance, depending on the nature of the work being undertaken. All five stages, however, are of equal importance. When planning work involving handling data, it is necessary to determine your intended learning outcome as to attempt to cover all aspects of all five elements is clearly impracticable. Handling data is an excellent example of mathematics to be used and applied in a wide range of circumstances. You will, however, need to teach the children before they can make their own decisions and choices.

> Think of handling data work that you have taught. How did you teach the knowledge, skills and understanding? Which elements of the five stages have you taught and did you teach them in the order of their progression (from question to answer)? Why? Have you always determined what was appropriate for the children or have you sometimes made it an objective of the lesson for the children to make their own decisions?
>
> What have you taught recently involving the children's engagement with handling data? What was its purpose? What was your intended learning outcome?

By now you may well have decided that you have not taught the five stages in order, but have probably concentrated on collecting and presenting the data. It is worth looking at each of these five stages, however, in order to determine how we can focus on the part they have to play in the whole. Eventually, of course, we are aiming to enable the children to progress independently through the whole process, making decisions throughout to enable them to answer their own questions satisfactorily.

Asking a question

One thing we know about children is that they ask questions. Sometimes these appear to be relevant and at other times not so relevant. In the realm of handling data, the potential questions that could be asked are wide ranging from all areas within and outside the curriculum. History, geography, science and PE all offer potential, as do PSHE and citizenship among others.

> Make a collection of questions the children ask over a week. How many of them could be used as a starting point for data collection? The question could be simple, requiring one set of data, or complex, requiring several sets of related data.
> Choose some of the questions suited to handling data. How else could the question have been worded? How could you use it?

As well as arising naturally, a good question can be specifically posed. It needs to be relevant and in context but not necessarily directly applicable – curiosity is a great motivator in children and intellectual stimulation should be promoted.

Making a plan

For teaching handling data, this planning stage is the basis of success. The types of questions will differ each time and in order to be able to answer them, the children need to draw up a good plan. Having been asked a question, you now need to determine what sort of data will help to answer it and how that data will be collected.

Consider your need as a teacher to have data that informs you about the progress the children have made. For example, reading progress over a year may be recorded through books read, cloze procedures, objectives met in shared reading, test results that may give reading ages or National Curriculum levels and application to written work.

> What data have you found it necessary to collect to inform the planning process in other areas of the curriculum? How much of the data is narrative? How much is numerical? How much has only one possibility and how much might be subject to experimental error (requiring repeated collection)? How much is easily collected and how did that factor influence your choice?

Within your lesson plan you will need to consider such things as:

- What do the children already know?
- What shall I have to teach that will be new?
- How much support will they need?
- How will I group them?
- What resources will I/they need?
- How will they record their data?
- How much time should I give them?

Once you have the answers, you can then plan how to teach the children to make a plan for their data gathering!

Collecting the data

Once the children have a good plan then this part should be relatively easy. Your own differentiated planning will determine how to manage this phase so that all children are able to take part and contribute at their own level.

Presenting the data

The management and manipulation of data to fit it for different purposes is an important part of the understanding that children should develop when learning about handling data. We can start from the first data organisational devices such as Venn and Carroll diagrams. According to which criteria are chosen, the children can draw different conclusions.

> Can you think of any examples of sorting that you have taught that could lead to different conclusions? Using a set of sorting objects (Logiblocks, Compare bears etc.) try to decide how many ways they can be sorted and what conclusions you might draw.

The exercise of sorting through different criteria should not only take place at the infant stage – data sorting can be used in a multitude of simple and complex ways to provide information to answer the question asked. This might result in a variety of presentations such as a graph or chart, calculated statistics or probability statements.

> Find some data work the children have done involving data presentation. Could the data have been presented in an alternative way? Would that have clarified or confused the findings?

Interpreting the data

If the previous four stages have been successfully completed, then this final stage of answering the original question should be easy. This completes the circle by going back to the original question posed and possibly generating new questions.

> What other questions arose out of the data collected other than the intended one(s)?

> When you last taught handling data, was it in a mathematics lesson or in another curriculum area? What connections were made? Did you teach through all five stages? How much of the decision-making was done by the children at each of the five stages? Can you break down what you did into the five stages?

Stage	Representation	Notation
1 Ask the question	e.g. How long would the daisy chain be if you made it using all the daisies on your playing field?	e.g.
2 Make a plan	e.g. We need to know: 1 How many daisies there are on the playing field. 2 How much each daisy adds to the chain. To do this we need to know, for 1: • how many daisies there are in a square metre (remember to repeat and average); • the area of the playing field; and for 2: • the average length of a chain with say 10 daisies – expect a range. Therefore, the class needs to be divided into at least six groups, preferably eight – 1 for field measuring, 3 for daisy counting and 4 for daisy chain-making (skill based).	e.g.
3 Collect the data	e.g. • Prepare counting squares and support materials for field measuring. • Decide where samples will be taken and means of recording. • Allocate tasks and collect.	e.g.
4 Present the data	e.g. • Calculate area of field. • Find mean of daisy count. • Calculate number of daisies on field. • Measure and find mean of daisy chains, then determine mean for 1 daisy.	e.g. • Draw plan with measures (scale or not?). • (Sample A + sample B + sample C) ÷ 3. • Area of field × mean daisy count = number of daisies. • (Length a + length b etc) ÷ number of chains, then ÷ 10 for one daisy.
5 Interpret the data	e.g. • Combine average length of daisy with calculated number of daisies to determine length of chain. • Relate this length to everyday experiences – number of times round the field, distance from school to church etc.	e.g. • Number of daisies on field × mean length for one daisy = length of daisy chain.

Figure 4.2

The children's learning

All five stages contribute to the development of the children's ability to make connections between various mathematical concepts and all sorts of other information available to them – whether taught as separate stages or as part of a whole.

The first stage – asking a question – contributes towards the development of analysis skills. The children learn how to adjust the framing of a question to allow it to be answered. They learn how key vocabulary can provide clues to the nature of data that is required and also how vocabulary can be misleading, so developing critical insight into the creative and flexible aspects of mathematics.

> How many ways during a school week, both within a mathematics lesson and otherwise, have the children in your class had opportunities to consider what they are asking when they pose a question and similarly, what you are asking when you ask a question? How do you know?

The second stage – planning – consolidates the understanding from the question stage. The children will have to resolve any residual lack of clarity in order to develop a working plan to answer the question. They will learn to think through the requirements of the question. This will help them learn to make connections with similar work undertaken previously. What do they already know and understand that they can apply to this particular situation and so find out what they want to know? This phase is an ideal opportunity for them to learn how the use of their own idiosyncratic jottings can help to develop clarity, support effective communication and so progress their learning.

> When the children are given a question to answer, how many different plans for appropriate data can they come up with, individually, in pairs or in groups? How can they learn to benefit from this type of exercise?

The third stage – collecting data – is a natural follow-on from the children's learning in the first and second stages but will not test the effectiveness of that learning – this comes when they reach the fourth and fifth stages. This third stage, however, offers opportunities to learn about such things as co-operative working, organisation of resources, recording techniques, reduction of experimental errors, and develops understanding of the approximate nature of measures.

> How does the arrangement of the groupings of the children contribute to the children's learning during this stage?

The fourth stage – presentation of the data – contributes the most to what is generally considered the mathematics part of handling data – graphs, percentages, averages and prediction. If the right decisions were made at the planning stage, the children will have the data they need. Now they will have the opportunity to learn how to present it so that the information required to answer the question is evident.

When considering your mathematics earlier in this chapter, you were asked the question: When you are presented with data, do you find it easier to interpret if it is in tabular, graphical or narrative form?

> Think about the children in your class. You will have offered them opportunities to answer questions posed through a variety of representations. How have you enhanced their ability to communicate their findings through verbal communication and other multi-sensory means?

At the fifth and final stage – interpreting the data – the children will be able to determine the effectiveness of their plan for answering the question. If they are able to answer the original question and explain how they can justify the answer, then their plan was effective. If they are still unsatisfied with the evidence they have, then of course they should have the opportunity to review their plan and make appropriate adjustments.

> In a recent lesson on handling data, how free did you feel to let the children learn from their evaluation of their own work? How was discussion used at each stage to enhance the children's learning?

Summary

- Handling data permeates everyday life and is a particularly useful aspect of real-life mathematics. Sometimes it is as simple as counting (in the early stages of Key Stage 1), other times it might involve quite complex applications (towards the end of Key Stage 2).

- Children who, through your teaching, engage regularly with some or all of the five equally important stages of handling data, have a simple but effective structure to adapt and apply whenever the need arises, whatever that need may be.

Processing, representing and interpreting

Introduction

An important part of handling data is from the point at which the children have data, either presented to them or collected themselves, which they have to process, represent and interpret to be able to answer the question originally posed. This chapter looks at the various ways that children can do this and the choices they should be encouraged to make.

In general, processing and representing of data is based on the comparison of one or more sets of data, which can be organised in different ways. These could include Venn and Carroll diagrams, charts, tables or graphs. When viewed in this way, the commonalities between the various forms become more evident. In tables, the intersection of columns and rows, representing two sets of data, enable the reader to determine a unique point and in graphs, the x and y axes do the same thing. Representation of more than two sets of data presents more of a challenge but is possible through colour, overlaying, multiple columns etc., all designed to simulate three-dimensional representations. It is important to remember that data needs to be presented in such a way that the questions can be answered; to do this it needs to be simple, clear, unambiguous and unbiased.

Your mathematics

Tables, charts and graphs

Data that is presented to us is usually processed in some way and the decision about appropriate form has already been taken. It is possible, however, to question this and to consider if a different presentation may be more suitable.

> Consider your teaching timetable. Is it organised with the days of the week on the rows or the columns? Which do you prefer? Why is it done this way? Does it matter?

> Now consider a train or bus timetable. Are the names of the stops in the rows or the columns? Where is time located? How does this relate to the convention on location of time with respect to the x or y axes in a graph?

Both tables and graphs have a title that tells you what information is contained under which conditions and headings for columns and rows or the axes. When considering tables, the choice of data to be displayed relates directly to the information needed and the title qualifies this. One example of this are SATS results, where data available might include:

- key stage;
- pupil name;
- year of test;
- subject;
- level achieved;
- gender;
- national data.

If, for example, we wanted to compare the results of the boys with those of the girls in the school, we would need several other sets of data to be able to make informed decisions. Figure 4.3 shows one possible arrangement into which the numbers of boys and girls achieving each level can be entered (is there a common denominator?). Another table would be needed if the progression of results over several years was considered relevant.

Table to compare the SATs results of boys and girls in this school for 2003																
	KS1								KS2							
	Ma				En				Ma			En			Sc		
Level	W	1	2	3	W	1	2	3	3	4	5	3	4	5	3	4	5
Boys		8	14	9													
Girls		4	16	9													

Figure 4.3

> How easy is this for you to understand? Do the doubled lines perform any useful purpose? How useful might the raw data be for comparison? How could it be better presented? What could be left out? What could be given in greater detail? What other ways can you think of to present the data in tabular form to enable an effective and useful comparison to be made?

Now think about graphs. The SATs information considered above could also be presented in the form of a bar chart which can be used when the data are in discrete categories.

> To address the previous question comparing the results of boys and girls, what would you put on your y axis? How does this relate to the table above? How might you organise the categories on the x axis? How does this relate to the choices you made earlier when determining the most effective table for you?

> Draw a bar chart using the data in Figure 4.3. How much information have you managed to include on one graph? What different questions can you answer from the information displayed? Consider Figure 4.4. How useful do you find a vertical combination of the data compared with horizontal comparisons?

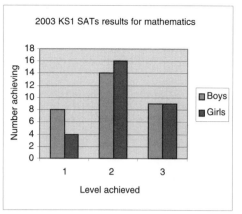
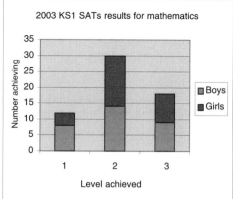

Figure 4.4

Does the presentation in Figure 4.5 make any more sense? Why or why not?

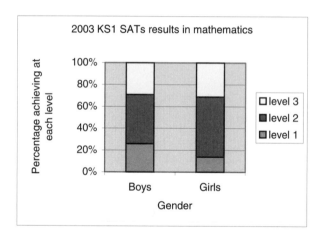

Figure 4.5

Compare your graph with the table(s) drawn up before. Which presentation do you prefer? Why? Which questions can you think of that are more easily answered with the table and which with the graph?

At this point it is worth considering another form of graphical presentation that offers visual comparisons of data. The bar graph arrangement above (Fig. 4.5), through translation to percentages, shows each level as a part of a whole. Figure 4.6 shows the same data presented as a pie chart demonstrating the same comparison.

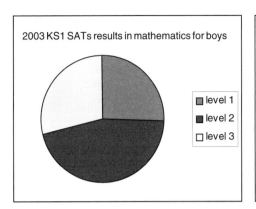

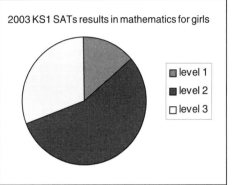

Figure 4.6

As you can see, for this presentation, two charts have been drawn – one for boys and one for girls.

> What do you prefer about this form of presentation? What do you not like as much as the bar chart?

> Could the pie charts be amalagamated? When considering several sets of data on one table or graph, at what stage does it become visually overloaded and therefore of less use?

ICT

ICT has greatly increased our ability to present data in a range of ways. It is still necessary to be discriminating about which forms are appropriate to the type of data and the intended purpose of the presentation.

> Consider the data-handling software available with which you are familiar.

ICT presents a wide range of possibilities for processing and representing data, some of which you may not have come across before.

How confident are you, in any given situation, of making an appropriate choice for the nature of the data you have? For example, if you wanted numerical information, would you choose a pie chart representation? (See again Figs 4.4, 4.5 and 4.6.) Are you confident that you would know when to use a line graph or a frequency graph? Which program gives you the most support when making decisions about processing and representing data?

Probability

Probability is included under the heading of handling data. One way to consider probability is that it takes the information provided by data and uses it to decide the likelihood of various events occurring. Consider again the SATs data from before (Fig. 4.3). Interpreting the distribution of the results from this year's data in this way, especially as shown in the pie chart representation, would suggest that next year, it is likely that more children will achieve Level 2 than either Levels 1 or 3. Further accuracy of prediction would be possible if the results from previous years were available, so that trends in distribution could be determined.

More precise determination of probability can be calculated numerically. Care must be taken to make judgements on the validity of the absolute value determined as it applies only to the data given and may not be directly applicable to future forecasting.

Take, for example, the probability noted above concerning the likelihood of children achieving Level 2 next year. From the chart in Figure 4.3, we can see that there are 60 children altogether and that 30 of them achieved Level 2. Clearly this can be seen as a half, so we could say that the probability for this occurring next year is a half ($^1/_2$, 0.5, 50%). As an indicator this is useful but there are several factors which will affect the outcome of next year's SATs.

What factors can you think of?

Based on the data given in Figure 4.3 from one year:

What is the probability of girls achieving Level 1?

What is the probability of boys achieving Level 1?

Calculation of this fraction from previous years' data will give a better indication of trend and a more accurate calculation can be made.

How useful would you find a numeric probability for prediction? Can you make the same predictions of trend from graphic representation?

Mean, mode, median and range

Data can also be processed statistically to give quantities that summarise features of the data, i.e. grouped into averages and ranges. The median, mode and mean are all versions of an average and serve different purposes. The range and interquartile ranges are connected with the median and together create a useful picture from the data. Using the small data sample created in the original table in Figure 4.3, it can be seen that:

	Boys	Girls
Median	2	2
Mode	2	2
Mean	2.03	2.17
Range	2	2
Lower quartile range	For data with this range, the interquartile ranges are not relevant	
Upper quartile range		

Figure 4.7

> How useful is this processed data? For what purpose? Why are the interquartile ranges not relevant here?

If you find these numbers to be of little use to you, there is another form of graph not yet considered – a box-whisker graph. This is a good example of data representation that seems to be rather underused and so is not well understood. It is, however, a visual presentation form of data such as medians and ranges that have been processed arithmetically and presented numerically and it is particularly useful for comparing the spread of data for two or more groups. Figure 4.8 is an example plotting test marks for eight groups.

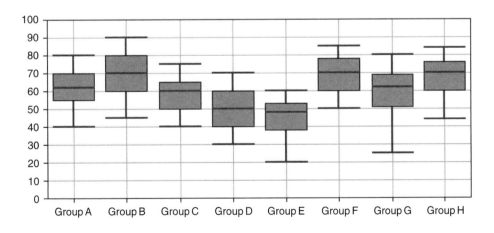

Figure 4.8

Which parts represent the median and the three ranges? Deconstruct the graph and present the information in a table. How useful do you find this visual representation compared with the numerical values?

Your teaching

Whether children generate their own data or it is presented to them, they need to be able to make judgements about the processing and representing to enable them to answer their questions through straightforward interpretation.

Venn and Carroll diagrams

One of the first ways you can teach children to sort data is through the use of Venn and Carroll diagrams. This allows them to deal with the concrete data and move it physically into the space where it fits, so avoiding abstraction when they are not able to deal with it. The Carroll diagram has been mentioned earlier as a chart that compares two or more sets of data, but in fact, the starting point for both Venn and Carroll diagrams is for just one set of objects which either fits (the universal set) or does not fit (the complement of the universal set) the given criteria, giving two subsets. For example, 'is blue or is not blue' or 'is a boy and is not a boy'. These practical activities translate easily into visual recording so the representation requires little new notation at this stage. Development of these principles to the consideration of two sets of criteria, or attributes, gives four subsets in both Venn and Carroll diagrams:

- has A but not B;
- has B but not A;
- has A and B;
- does not have A and does not have B.

Children can start to make decisions about which diagram to use and how to label the fields. Deconstruction is also an important teaching strategy. An unlabelled Venn or Carroll diagram with the data already sorted, either by you or by another group of children, can encourage a child to think about what the chosen attributes are. As a development, an error could be used to further challenge the children.

How can you use a Venn diagram for three sets of attributes? How many subsets does this make available? Is it possible to use a Venn diagram to represent more than three sets of attributes?

One interesting aspect of this sorting is that it introduces the idea of categorical data in which the boundaries are definite. But statements concerned with colour of hair or eyes, for example, sometimes cannot be determined as 'is and is not'. These provide opportunities for discussion with children throughout the primary age range.

> Can you think of other 'grey' areas for classification?

As mentioned before, data presented to us is usually sorted in some way. When children collect their own data, you need to decide how much directional input they require from you and how much they should be left to their own devices. Children usually either note each piece of information as they collect it or have some kind of system to sort as they collect.

For example, for a school survey to determine favourite breakfast cereals, the data could be collected such that:

- the name of each cereal is noted as each child says it, culminating in a long list – Wheatybangs, Corncracks, Wheatybangs, Riceypops, Riceypops, Wheatybangs, Corncracks, Riceypops, Wheatybangs, Corncracks etc.

or

- an initial discussion could determine the common favourites and then either:
  - a chart with column headings or
  - a block graph with labels on the x axis

could be prepared. Each child's contribution in the survey could then be entered in the appropriate column at the point of collection.

> What is the teaching advantage of letting the children collect their data in the way they devise? What are the disadvantages?

It is worth considering here some of the notations and representations used at this stage and the need for consistency.

Data collected in charts is normally recorded using tallying. While we should always encourage children to develop their own idiosyncratic methods (i.e. jottings), the standardisation of this notation form enables the data to be read by everyone without ambiguity and introduces the idea of effective communication. The standard tallying system, as illustrated in Figure 4.9, enables totalling at the end to be achieved through counting in 5s or pairs of 5s, i.e. 10s.

| ~~HHT~~ ~~HHT~~ ~~HHT~~ ~~HHT~~ II | Total is: 5, 10, 15, 20, **22** |

Or

| ~~HHT~~ ~~HHT~~
~~HHT~~ ~~HHT~~
II | Total is: 10, 20, **22** |

Figure 4.9

The other decision that children have to make when drawing up graphs as suggested here is whether to label the lines or the spaces on both *x* and *y* axes.

> Consider the favourite cereal example above. How could you teach the children that they need to label the spaces on the *x* axis but the lines on the *y* axis?

The decision about axes involves not only how to label the intervals but also how to label the *x* axis and the *y* axis. Sometimes this decision is determined by convention. For example, as we have seen, categorical data names are placed on the *x* axis as are other data that can be measured at regular intervals, such as goals scored or group boundaries (discussed further later) and any measures associated with time.

> How would you teach children how to make decisions about labelling the *x* axis?

Scales

Figure 4.10 shows two possible bar charts of the results of the cereal survey. It can be seen that to include each individual count on the *y* axis is unmanageable. The chart on the right has an interval of 5, which means that, while it is not possible to have each total meeting a line, it does provide a much clearer picture.

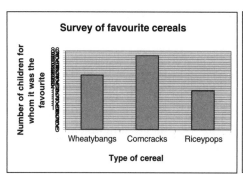
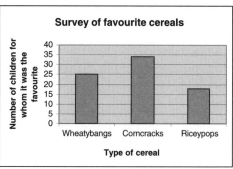

Figure 4.10

The introduction of scales as a reasonable way to clarify the picture helps when children are then taught other areas of mathematics, e.g. scales on measuring equipment. The division of each part into 2 or 5 or 10 has relevance when the alternative is considered. The judgement of actual value is then much more easily made as children have a context within which to try to visualise the divisions that are not drawn. In the example above, the number of children that favour Corncracks can be seen to be more than 30 but less than 35. The top of the bar is closer to the 35 than the 30 so it is reasonable to decide that its value is probably 33 or 34.

> How could you adjust this graph to improve the accuracy of the reading?

Pie charts are another useful way of representing discrete data for making visual comparisons, but the need to calculate fractions of 360° and then draw the segments accurately has previously been a barrier to the expectation for children to produce their own. There are ways of producing pie charts which avoid using awkward calculations, such as circles divided into 100 to give percentage divisions and providing children with totals that are simple equivalent fractions of 360. The latter, however, does not reflect the data that is likely to be collected by the children. But since the introduction of ICT as a resource for learning, children have been able to generate pie charts easily so making the production of this type of chart possible from a much earlier stage.

The children could produce a pie chart of their cereal survey, allowing them to make an immediate visual judgement on relative proportion.

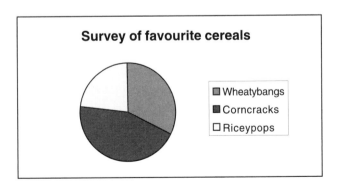

Figure 4.11

> Compare this pie chart with the bar chart. When teaching, how would you develop the children's understanding of the merits and drawbacks of each?

As the data that the children will be asked to deal with becomes more sophisticated, they can be introduced to the idea of grouping the data before presenting it to provide a less complex picture. Tallying groups count in 5s, but each of the individual counts is still evident and counts of less than five can be specified. Another way children could represent a large amount of data is by using a pictogram (Fig. 4.12). This develops the block graph of the cereal survey from a one-for-one representation to a symbol to represent any sized count. Unlike tallying, it is not possible in a pictogram to determine the size of a part as a part symbol merely means less than the whole.

If one car represents every 20 cars counted, then in this survey between 61 and 79 were counted.

Figure 4.12

Another example of representing grouped data is answering a question on how the heights of children differ according to age. Data on height and age would be collected for all the children in the school.

> How would you teach the children to devise their own recording table to answer a question about height and age?

The age could be recorded in years. It is important to note that this is a grouping method as one child might be celebrating his sixth birthday on the day of the survey and another might be looking forward to his seventh birthday the next day, but they would both be recorded as six years old.

Similarly the height could be recorded in individual centimetres or included in a group representing 5 centimetres (Fig. 4.13). The notation for recording this group needs to include the start and end of the group without overlap (the continuous nature of measures is discussed elsewhere).

Grouping in fives, to a whole centimetre	
90–94	ЖII
95–99	ЖI ЖII
100–104	ЖI ЖII I
105–109	etc.
etc.	

Figure 4.13

This could also be represented in a way that means introducing another form of notation.

≤90 – <95
≤95 – <100
≤100 – <105
≤105 – <110
etc.

Figure 4.14

But this does not mean the same as Figure 4.13.

> In which ways is it different? In which circumstances would Figure 4.13 be suitable and in which Figure 4.14? What are the similarities and differences between pictograms and the two forms of grouped data?

Much mathematical understanding can be developed through discussion and questioning and this can inform choices that have to be made about representation and notation.

> How would you teach the children to use each of the above forms of notation and then develop their understanding so that they are able to make appropriate choices?

We have not considered line graphs or scattergrams so far. Line graphs extend the plots made for each piece of data by joining the plots with lines. It is still only the actual plots that count as they reflect actual data, but the lines give a picture of the trends shown by the data. Line graphs are generally associated with continuous data, so much of what is recorded as a result of measure can be represented this way, for example time (in particular), height and mass.

> Can you think of data that should not be presented in a line graph? How could you teach the difference to children?

Scattergrams offer another opportunity for visual interpretation. Unlike pie charts, they are easily produced on squared or graph paper. The main feature of the scattergram is to provide an indication of strength of trend when two sets of data are compared when looking for a connection, or correlation, between them. The data needs to be paired – comparing the heights of children with their age lends itself ideally to this. The scattergram allows children to make comparative statements of trend such as 'the older the child the taller'. Drawing a line of best fit, without ICT assistance, is a bit hit and miss, which is why these graphs are not often used at primary level.

However, try this. Hold (or get a friend to hold) the graph, with its crosses, at arm's length or further away and squint so the graph becomes fuzzy. If a reasonable line of best fit is possible, the crosses will merge and the path of the line can be estimated and drawn. From this the children can make deductions about such evidence as anomalous results and the closeness and validity of the fit. If a data-handling program to produce the scattergram is used, then the computer will draw the line of best fit.

> How could you display other information on the scattergram, for comparison, such as gender trends?

Probability

In the primary school we are not expected to teach numeric calculation of probability, but it is a valuable way to make connections between fractions, decimals, percentages, ratio and proportion. The children encounter probability in everyday life such as:

- It is likely that half the children will be unable to get to school because of the snow.
- There is a 1 in 10 chance of winning a raffle prize.

There are also some misconceived perceptions of probability such as:

- It's much harder to throw a six than any of the other numbers.
- I've already thrown heads twice so it must be tails next time.

Some experience of the workings of probability to develop theoretical understanding using familiar occurrences – coins, dice, playing cards etc. – help the children to understand more of how probability is determined and can challenge their understanding.

One example of this could be a discussion about the likelihood of an event happening through placing on a probability line. Is it ever right to say something is certain or impossible? What judgements and compromises do we have to make?

It is reasonable to decide that a 'fair' coin could land either heads up or tails up with equal probability. That is, the probability of either event occurring is a half (in several fraction forms), or even, or 50 : 50. Interestingly, one notation of a half is $\frac{1}{2}$ or one out of two possibilities, whereas the notation for evens is 1 : 1, sayling one event compared with one other event gives a total of two possible events.

> Consider a die (a 'fair' one, of course). How many different ways could children express the probability of throwing a three? How could the notation of these representations be explained?

The combinations possible when two events are linked together is worth presenting to children to help clarify their understanding, but this should be kept to events that the children can see and experiment with to illustrate the theory directly. An example of this is tossing two coins. A not unreasonable assumption usually made would be that they would land either heads and heads, tails and tails or one of each, suggesting the probability of each event occurring to be $^1/_3$ or $1:2$. Gathering data through experimentation would enable the children to compare their theory with the evidence of the data, while learning to take account of experimental error, e.g. throwing a die 36 times will theoretically result in six of each number. The children will, however, probably find they have different results. A greater number of throws will reduce the effect of experimental error.

> Over 100 tosses of the two coins together, the children might *think* the tally would be about one third both heads, one third both tails and one third a head and a tail. The results would actually show that twice as many fell with a head and a tail as fell with both heads or both tails. How is this explained by the theory?

The theory underlying the principles of AND and OR when two events are combined is discussed in Chapter 5 with reference to computer search engines. It is worth allowing the children to consider what the effect might be of asking for the probabilities of, for example, throwing two dice and looking for:

- a 3 OR a 4;
- a 3 AND a 4.

> What are the probabilities of each of these? Why does the AND give a smaller probability than the OR?

> Think of other probability theory and practice the children could undertake for one or two events using dice and standard playing cards.

The children's learning

At all times, the discussion associated with the decisions made along the way are invaluable as teaching and learning strategies. Whether children are presented with data that has already been processed in some way or whether they generate their own, the choice of processing and representing is an integral part to developing understanding and the ability to apply their knowledge and skills in different mathematical and curricular areas. The children will also learn about applying conventions and determining their relevance.

Effective learning is achieved both through explicit teaching of each skill and scrap of knowledge and through children experimenting and developing by trial and improvement. These later stages of the whole handling data process offer opportunities for both. If processing, representing and interpreting is taught as an interconnection of a range of types and purposes, children can make informed decisions and be in control of their understanding and hence learning.

Summary

- Handling data is an area of mathematics that we meet all the time.
- Usually, data is presented to us in a form that the producers believe will lead us to draw their intended conclusions.
- Understanding of the ways in which data can be processed and represented, to this end, will encourage children to be objective about both data they are given and data that they generate themselves.

CHAPTER 5

Cross-curricular connections

Introduction

Throughout this book, reference has been made to the use of mathematics in other curriculum areas and the map of connections (see p. xi) supports this.

Recent primary education history has fluctuated between a policy of a fully integrated curriculum in which all work is linked through the different subject areas and the policy of subjects being taught as entirely discrete entities. Within this, schools were given guidelines about the proportion of the teaching day to be allocated to each subject, which might have been interpreted as requiring more time than there was available. The present curriculum retains a balance that puts some of the teaching day aside for the teaching of core subjects and the balance for the foundation subjects. Local education authorities (LEAs) and schools interpret this individually according to their own particular guidelines and requirements.

School timetables have been established to enable schools to cover the curriculum in the most effective way. While this book is not the forum for discussion on definitions of what this means from political, sociological, educational or economic perspectives, you will be involved with trying to teach as effectively as possible within the understanding defined by your LEA, your school and your own personal philosophy of education.

> What is your experience of the arrangement of the school timetable? Why has it been done this way? What do you think about this?

One of the considerations for the teaching of mathematics is the knowledge that, of all subjects in the curriculum, it seems to have the greatest capacity to be disliked and for children and adults to believe that they are poor at it. What is more, this is not necessarily viewed by many people as a problem in the way that, for example, poor literacy skills are seen. Yet outside the school, the lines of distinction between subjects is rarely made absolute and a great deal involves mathematics in either a numeric or a problem-solving role.

Consider such everyday activities as:

- choosing a birthday present;
- catching a bus;
- sorting laundry;
- riding a bike;
- making breakfast;
- playing at a dolls' tea party.

If we think of the first, choosing a birthday present, the various processes involved can be outlined, for example:

- Who is the receiver – age, gender, interests, relationship to you?
- Time you have available to shop – how far you can/are willing to travel.
- Means of delivery – post, courier, deliver personally.
- Budget.
- Possibility of consultation – inside information, a friend to help with ideas.

This is not, of course, a definitive list – just some ideas. If each of the processes is examined, only the budget seems to have any direct link with any of the primary curriculum subjects, i.e. mathematics. Another way of analysing these processes might be through classification into knowledge, skills or understanding. For example, information about the receiver requires knowledge about him/her from a variety of perspectives and the understanding to realise the implications of this knowledge in the frame of buying a birthday present.

Look back at the list of activities. For any one (or one of your own):

- break it down into separate processes;
- decide which subjects in the primary curriculum are represented;
- consider whether knowledge, skills and/or understanding are required to successfully complete each process.

The exercises above reinforce the presence of mathematics in almost every activity, even if only in a very small way. In many schools, teachers use opportunities to practise directly related mathematics, both mental and written. For example, when registering children are asked:

How many are there normally in the class?
How many are away today?
So how many are there here today?

If there are 30 here today, and 20 are having school meals, how many are not?
What fraction of the class is this?
Therefore what fraction are having school meals?

> Think of your daily timetable. Which parts are not timetabled for direct teaching? What would you be doing in those times? What directly related mathematics might you be able to ask the children to undertake at that time?

It is not the intention of this chapter to list lessons in which cross-curricular links to mathematics can be made. It is important, however, that it is seen as an integral part of every subject in school rather than solely as a discrete, mysterious subject that is waiting to catch you out! The phrase 'use it or lose it' applies to everything we learn and therefore, through repeated application in a variety of different settings, mathematical learning is over-learned and reinforced. Demystification through familiarity will go a long way to promote a positive image of mathematics.

There is also an interesting argument about the value of incidental, non-explicit learning when compared with directly taught and identified learning. Mathematics taught within other subjects may or may not be identified as mathematics to the children. If the children are made aware each time of mathematics in its multifarious uses, they may accept it more easily than if it is only taught discretely. Alternatively they may become more flexible in its applications if it is included as a part of the other subject without being specifically identified. One version of a popular wisdom among teachers is that:

- if we hear, we forget;
- if we see, we remember;
- if we do, we understand.

But if we 'do', without conscious focus on the underlying purpose to the activity, how well do we learn?

> As a teacher, you need to identify when and what mathematics is included in any lesson. But do you feel that the children should be told that it is mathematics or that it is part of the lesson?

The core subjects

English

The role of language in developing confidence and competence in mathematics has been a central theme throughout this book. While the first part of this chapter has encouraged you to see how mathematics pervades everything, it has to be acknowledged that language is central. Any language limitation inhibits progress in mathematics and sometimes creates incorrect impressions of a child's mathematical ability. One possibility is to use mathematics to support development in reading and writing rather than vice versa. Consider, for example, the choice of a book for reading. We make many judgements during the process of choosing such as:

- the thickness of the book;
- the size of the font;
- the length of the words;
- the amount of words on the page;
- the number of pages in the book;
- the proportion of words and pictures.

These give us indications, based on previous experiences, about:

- the time it would take to read it;
- the speed at which we would be able to read it;
- our probable enjoyment of the reading experience;
- the value for money.

We also make judgements such as having read just over halfway and whether we can stay awake long enough to finish it.

Making explicit these subconscious indicators will contribute to a child's awareness of their progress in reading and how they can take more control over this. Thus mathematics applied in this way becomes a tool.

The language of mathematics has been discussed in the preceding chapters. One of the key points worth reiterating here is the different ways in which terms and vocabulary are sometimes used in everyday as well as mathematical usage.

Science

Science links in many ways with mathematics at several levels. The requirements of scientific enquiry are very similar to those of mathematical investigation. Information is collected that will enable the children to reach conclusions. The latter stages of the process require that the data are collected, presented and interpreted in ways that enable conclusions to be drawn.

Scientific experimentation includes an expectation of error and the reduction of the effect of this error. Mathematics helps in this process. Children need to examine the data to make judgements about the extent of the errors and the effect on the results. Repetition of experiments is a basic tenet of scientific investigation as it allows anomalous results to be detected and accounted for, and also for averages (means) to be determined as a further device for reduction of the effects of experimental error.

The presentation of findings is part of this and can range from simple tabulation and examination for anomalous results to results presented in scattergrams where validity can be judged through reference to line of best fit.

> Consider science work about forces. You may, for example, wish the children to investigate the effects of friction. A fairly standard scenario for this is objects and ramps. What variables or factors might you encourage the children to explore? For each, what might you expect the children to do in terms of:
>
> - presentation of findings;
> - determination of experimental error (including appropriate degree of accuracy of results);
> - reduction of experimental error.
>
> What mathematics is involved from both the problem-solving and the calculation perspectives?

> Try this process for other science topics. What about food, magnetism, sound, pondlife, temperature or materials?

ICT can be used to support science and the mathematics in science. Much of the management of information gathered, described above, can be developed through the use of appropriate data-handling programs. However, ICT can also be used for the earlier stage of data gathering. Data capture hardware can reduce experimental error through human intervention. For example, readings for reduction of temperature over time. The use of light detection switches can enable parachute fall times to be much more accurately measured than manually operated stopwatch. Pulse monitors eliminate the often tortuous process of obtaining pulse rates before and after exercise. In all of these examples, the data collected can then be processed mathematically for interpretation.

> Look at the science National Curriculum. In which ways can ICT be used as part of the experimental process of data gathering? How can ICT be used to process the data? When is mathematics not an appropriate part of the work?

The foundation subjects

The foundation subjects can, for the purpose of this chapter, be grouped into:

- Humanities – history, geography, religious education (RE), citizenship, personal, social and health education (PSHE), modern foreign languages (MFL).

- Art – art, design technology (DT).
- Ourselves – physical education (PE), drama, music.

Clearly there are overlaps and none is discrete as through them all, the children are learning about themselves and their relationships with others.

Humanities

The humanities deal with the lives and beliefs of others and ourselves, both past and present. The mathematics within this includes factual and statistical information which is determined from a range of sources and which may also have a mathematical basis for interrogation. Reference books provide the reader with contents and index pages that enable the relevant part to be found efficiently. Even the basic skills and understanding of the recognition of numbers and their relative order enables readers to: find the reference; open the book at about the right place; look at the number of the page they have opened; decide whether they need to go forwards or backwards from there and by how much, and from there find the page they require.

Web searches

Increasingly, children research information using the World Wide Web (www). Search engines use Boolean principles (noted in Ch. 4) to process the search information given and so provide relevant sites. Children who have a basic understanding of probability will have a better understanding of this search device or vice versa. In this situation, once again there is the potential for misconceptions through the crossover of language from everyday to mathematical and then within mathematics itself. Normally, when we use the word 'and' we mean something like 'as well' or 'in addition' and then of course 'add'. But in probability and hence search terms AND reduces possibility. Similarly, we tend to accept the use of the word 'or' to mean the opposite, such as 'either, or but not both'. But in probability, the use of the term OR increases possibility.

For example: if I were to use a search engine to find out about chocolate AND chickens, it would find all references that contain both words. But if I were to input chocolate OR chickens, the search engine would give me all references with chocolate, all with chickens and of course, all with both. Therefore I would have a great many more using the OR instruction than I would with the AND.

Understanding of this principle enables children to search much more efficiently and effectively.

Choose an aspect of one of the humanities from the National Curriculum. Try your favourite search engine to see how efficient you can make your search for relevant data.

The information gleaned from these searches is often of a statistical nature about the people being studied. Much of this can be used by the children to make comparisons about the people being studied and their own lives. For example, in geography the children may compare population density in a contrasting location with that of their own; in history, they may compare the population of their own location in the past with now; and in RE they may compare the populations with one religious belief with their own.

Use the National Curriculum to determine what statistical information children may collect when studying various topics in geography, history and RE.

The presentation of the statistics may vary according to who compiled it and for what purpose it was originally intended. One skill that children can develop is that of reordering information into a configuration that is of most use to them. This may take several forms across the various groups in the class and in itself is a basis for discussion. Population data can be offered in a variety of ways such as means, bar charts and comparative words in a narrative, all of which enable children to understand the differences and similarities presented. For historical events data, a timeline may help provide a perspective; some children may relate better to a comparative scale, such as relating the Stone Age to now to a single day; or again a narrative may be of the most use to another group.

Select one of the humanities topics considered before and the data you collected in your search. How was that data presented to you? How useful did you find it in that form? How else could it be organised and present a clear picture of the information it gives?

History

Mathematics is also necessary for interpreting data that the children collect for themselves through surveys, censuses and questionnaires. The skills learned through the interrogation of already prepared data will help them to make their own decisions as to what will be useful for them, how to collect it and how to present it. An example of the data available to children is the gravestones in the local churchyard and parish records. This could be considered morbid but is a rich source of local information and generally of interest to the children. The information might include: dates of birth and death, and hence life length; family members and relations; family histories; causes of death; marriages and baptisms.

> What mathematics could you plan into a study of this nature?

Geography

In geography, other mathematically relevant topics might embrace mapping skills, including:

- scale, distances (relative and actual), direction;
- contours and isobars;
- latitude and longitude, including projections, grid references, time zones and seasonal changes.

> What mathematics is involved in these? What others can you think of?

RE

In RE, as in history, dates are important. Each religion has its festivals and these are located within the year, either as fixed dates or as a particular day within a month, as in Christmas Day, or through astronomical calculations such as Easter, which is the first Sunday after the first full moon following the 21st of March, and the Hindu festival of Holi, which is celebrated on the day after the full moon in early March every year. To this can also be added the large number of non-religious festivals celebrated around the world.

An additional facet is that some religions have different calendars from each other and so dates of festivals may appear to be different year by year when compared with the Western calendar but are actually fixed. For example, Yom Kippur is a Jewish festival that falls on the 10th day of the 7th month in the Jewish calendar, which is different from the Western calendar. As noted in Chapter 3, the measurement of time is complex and is only really marked by the imposition of a human construct, which is generally arbitrary although often tied in with some historical or religious event. The recent discussion about the significance of the passing of the millennium raised two points:

- Should the new millennium have been marked when the numbers denoting the century changed from 19 to 20 or when the new century (and hence millennium) actually started (i.e. 2001, as 2000 marked the last year of the old millennium)?
- The date marking the start was determined as a necessary standardisation and was based on the birth of Christ. However, evidence shows it is not the actual

date and therefore the year 2000 is similarly an administrative convenience of no significance, astronomically, religiously or otherwise. Indeed, taking this one step further, if we had nine fingers on our hands instead of ten, then the year 2000 would have come a great deal earlier than it did.

These discussions are invaluable as teaching tools to enable children to engage with the fallibility and creativity of our uses of numbers.

> When preparing your next medium-term plan for RE, how could you incorporate this aspect of dates and what mathematics might it involve? Can you think of any other subject-specific mathematics within history and RE?

Citizenship, PSHE and MFL

Consider citizenship and PSHE – in many ways, the preceding discussion fits these areas of developing children's understanding of human lives. Simple mathematical cross-references related to such ideas as sharing, equality and value can be an integral part of circle time or class discussions, with the mathematics being evident or not depending on how you have chosen to plan it.

> Can you think of any other ways that mathematics can be included and integrated into these alternative perspectives of the humanities?

Modern foreign languages offer opportunities to develop the children's understanding of counting systems. In English, the regularisation of counting occurs in the teens, although the daily usage over many years has changed 'eight and ten' into 'eighteen'. Having contracted 'two tens' into 'twenty', 'three tens' into 'thirty' and so on, the counting falls into a regular pattern that can be directly translated into place value notation. However, young children may experience difficulty distinguishing 'forty' from 'fourteen' when spoken. This issue does not arise in languages that have a different structure.

> Compare some of the common languages of Europe. What patterns in counting are common with those of the English language? What are the differences? How do these avoid the confusion mentioned above? Why might these be?

Arts

DT and art

There is much mathematics within DT and art. The design and strength of a construction often relies upon shape, apparent in everyday objects such as pylons and footballs. For example, the main shape in a pylon is the triangle, for strength, and a stool with three legs will never wobble.

> Which shapes are there in a traditional football and how many are there of each? Could you design a football using different amounts of these shapes or using other shapes? What shapes can you identify in other constructions around you?

We encourage children to plan and for this, scale, ratio, symmetry, balance and proportion play an important part, which requires understanding and application of mathematics as well as the skills of calculation and use of the relevant equipment. The sort of examination and deconstruction considered above enables children at the planning stage to begin their design from a knowledgeable base. Another example in art is the exploration of the golden ratio through the examination of existing art, which can provide models for the children's work that they can then apply to their own work. Trial and improvement strategies through piloting plans and designs until they achieve one that they can use for their final product consolidates their understanding of their earlier analysis.

As with many things, effective planning in the early stages allows better progress to be made during the later stages and also enables evaluation. Planning does not just involve preparing a design – children need to decide what materials they want and how much and the nature of this material will depend upon the purpose it has to serve, availability and ease of use.

> Consider an art or DT topic you have recently planned or taught. What mathematics might be involved at the planning stage to improve progress in the later stages? What mathematics might be included to contribute to the development of mathematical understanding through application?

Drama, music and PE

Drama and PE, including dance, involve the children learning more about their body and how to manage it. Music, while not directly connected with the body, could be considered to have a direct influence upon children physically and emotionally. Counting, again, is a foundation to much work in PE and music. There has been much staffroom discussion about a possible connection between ability in music and mathematics. Certainly, pattern forms a significant part of the concepts that underlie both these subjects and has been discussed from a mathematical viewpoint elsewhere in this book.

Drama

Teachers use drama as a means of expression that enables children to become absorbed in the subject through personal interaction with mind, body and emotions. As such, it crosses all subjects and rather than considering mathematics within drama, it is worth reflecting upon drama within mathematics. Children taking on roles as physical resources stimulates insights into how the mathematics works through engagement at several levels. Some examples of this might be:

- Being a robot to imitate movement, both linear and turning.
- Being part of a calculation machine for demonstration of the concepts underlying the four basic operations such as:
  - addition through simple aggregation or augmentation;
  - subtraction through removal or comparison;
  - multiplication through repeated addition or 'lots of';
  - division through grouping or sharing.
- Role-play for various money-using scenarios.
- Assuming a digit role to show the dynamics of multiplying or dividing by multiples of ten.

> Make a list of other drama-based learning that you have used. What others can you think of?

Music

Consider music – we may encounter many types of music and the connections between them are more apparent in some cases than in others.

> - What patterns can be found in traditional childhood music such as nursery rhymes? How do the patterns repeat? How do they change?
> - How do these patterns develop through into folk songs and music?
> - Is it a similar development into popular music from the charts?
> - What number connections have you considered?

> Listen to a favourite piece of music from one of the older classical composers, such as Bach. What patterns can you hear there? Are they similar to the patterns previously found?

> Now listen to a piece from a more recent composer. Can you still find the patterns? How similar are they? How much have they been adjusted? Can you still find the numbers in the patterns?

Floor robots and mobile phones have the capability of being programmed to play tunes using simple numerical values for tones, halftones and note length.

> How does this work?

Up to this point we have only considered the evidence of our ears. But music uses graphic representation of the patterns as a universal language that enables any musician to reproduce the composer's intentions. When we look at a score, the musical notation for the time signature tells us how many beats in the bar and the length of each of those beats.

> How could this lead to confusion and possible misconceptions in fractions?

Understanding of the notation for the notes enables the musician to be able to tell through positional clues, whether a note is higher or lower than the preceding one, which note to play or sing and how long that note should last. Within a bar, the total length of the notes written should be the same as indicated by the time signature.

> What connections does this have with basic counting and number work? How is this of use when more than one part is being played or sung at the same time?

Dance

Dance uses the patterns from music. Folk, or country, dancing has its own music to which the choreographers decide which steps and moves the dancers should use. Of course, the origins of the older dances, as with the music, cannot always be traced as they have evolved over generations and so are not choreographed. These same, usually simple, counting patterns in these naturally evolved dances from all lands are reflected in more complex and contrived music and dance.

> What mathematics would children be using when composing their own music or choreographing their own dances?

PE and games

Consideration of a games lesson shows less obvious mathematical connections. Patterns can be found, for example, in the formations in team play, calculations in the division of the number of balls between the number of children in the class and estimation of the time available for each group to plan, rehearse and show their work. These are all valid and should be used as incidental use of mathematics in the lesson. Of more relevant, explicit use may be the keeping and analysis of scores. Runs scored within a 15-minute innings for each team can form the basis for a league table, batting averages and run rates. On a less competitive note, this information can be used to calculate how far each batter ran or how long players were sitting out waiting for their turn.

> Think of other games, such as tennis. What mathematics might occur incidentally? What might you plan into the lesson?

Summary

- Cross-curricular links in mathematics can be incidental or a specific part of the lesson. Either way, teachers need to plan them in.

- Mathematics needs a positive image and one way to achieve this is to help children to accept it as a normal and relevant part of every aspect of their schooling. If it is not seen as a problem or something to be feared, then it will not become so.

- In addition to planning (of key importance) for creative teaching and learning of mathematics that acknowledges its fallibility, you need to feel confident and competent about your teaching to be a positive role model to your colleagues and the parents and carers of the children.

Bibliography

Askew, M., Brown, M., Rhodes, V. and Wiliam, D. (1997) *Effective Teachers of Numeracy: Report*. London: TTA.

Chinn, S. and Ashcroft, R. (1998) *Mathematics for Dyslexics: A Teaching Handbook*. London: Whurr.

Cockcroft, W. H. (1982) *Mathematics Counts*. London: HMSO.

DfEE (1999) *National Numeracy Strategy*. London: DfEE.

DfEE/QCA (1999) *The National Curriculum: Handbook for Primary Teachers in England*. London: HMSO.

DfEE/QCA (2000) *Curriculum Guidance for the Foundation Stage*. London: DfEE.

DfES (2001) *Using Assess and Review Lessons*. London: DfES.

DfES (2003) *Excellence and Enjoyment*. London: DfES.

DfES http://www.standards.dfes.gov.uk/numeracy/prof_dev/ (accessed 2 June 2003)

Gatsby Technical Education Project (1997) http://www.gtep.co.uk/~gtep-co.uk/public_html/gtep/maths_primary.html www.ex.ac.uk/cimt/mepres/

Haylock, D. (2001) *Mathematics Explained for Primary Teachers*. London: Sage.

Haylock, D. and Cockburn, A. (2003) *Understanding Mathematics in the Lower Primary Years*. London: Paul Chapman.

Liebeck, P. (1990) *How Children Learn Mathematics*. Harmondsworth: Penguin.

National Numeracy Strategy (NNS) (1999) *Mathematical Vocabulary*. London: DfEE.

National Numeracy Strategy (NNS) (2002) *Learning from Mistakes and Misconceptions in Mathematics*. London: DfES.

Skemp, R. (1991) *Mathematics in the Primary School*. London: Taylor and Francis.

Vygotsky, L. (1978) *Mind in Society*. Cambridge, Mass.: MIT Press.

Supplementary reading

Fox, B., Montague-Smith, A. and Wilkes, S. (2001) *Using ICT in Primary Mathematics: Practice and Possibilities*. London: David Fulton.

Hopkins, C., Gifford, S. and Pepperell, S. (1996) *Mathematics in the Primary School*. London: David Fulton.

Hughes, M., Desforges, C., Mitchell, C. with Carré, C. (2000) *Numeracy and Beyond: Applying Mathematics in the Primary School*. Buckingham: OUP.

Mooney, C., Ferne, L., Fox, S., Hansen, A. and Wrathmell, R. (2000) *Primary Mathematics, Knowledge and Understanding*. Exeter: Learning Matters.

Mooney, C., Briggs, M., Fletcher, M. and McCullouch, J. (2001) *Primary Mathematics: Teaching Theory and Practice*. Exeter: Learning Matters.

Suggate, J., Davis, A. and Goulding, M. (2001) *Mathematical Knowledge for Primary School Teachers*. London: David Fulton.

The following may be useful when considering learning styles and modes

Jacques, K. and Hyland, R. (eds) (2000) *Professional Studies: Primary Phase*. Exeter: Learning Matters.

Riding, R. and Rayner, S. (1998) *'Learning Styles' Cognitive Styles and Learning Strategies: Understanding Difference in Learning and Behaviour*. London: David Fulton.

Index